How to Negotiate Book

CRAFTED BY SKRIUWER

Copyright © 2024 by Skriuwer.

All rights reserved. No part of this book may be used or reproduced in any form whatsoever without written permission except in the case of brief quotations in critical articles or reviews.

For more information, contact : **kontakt@skriuwer.com** (www.skriuwer.com)

TABLE OF CONTENTS

CHAPTER 1: INTRODUCTION TO NEGOTIATION BASICS

- *Definition of negotiation and everyday examples*
- *Why negotiation skills matter for problem-solving*
- *Key elements of a successful negotiation*

CHAPTER 2: SETTING CLEAR OBJECTIVES

- *Deciding on main goals, fallback plans, and priorities*
- *Realistic expectations and walk-away points*
- *Organizing objectives for better focus*

CHAPTER 3: RESEARCH AND INFORMATION GATHERING

- *Collecting market data and relevant facts*
- *Validating sources and dealing with conflicting information*
- *Using research to strengthen credibility*

CHAPTER 4: PREPARATION TOOLS AND TECHNIQUES

- *Checklists, role-playing, and mental rehearsal*
- *Choosing the meeting format and location*
- *Planning openings, questions, and backup strategies*

CHAPTER 5: COMMUNICATION FUNDAMENTALS

- *Clarity in speech, tone, and word choice*
- *Building rapport through respectful language*
- *Avoiding misunderstandings in verbal exchanges*

CHAPTER 6: LISTENING SKILLS

- *Active listening vs. merely hearing*
- *Barriers to good listening and how to overcome them*
- *Encouraging the other side to speak openly*

CHAPTER 7: BODY LANGUAGE IN NEGOTIATIONS

- *Recognizing posture, eye contact, and facial cues*
- *Mirroring and matching for better rapport*
- *Managing nervous gestures and controlling nonverbal signals*

CHAPTER 8: BUILDING TRUST AND CREDIBILITY

- *Honesty, consistency, and showing expertise*
- *Being transparent about capabilities and intentions*
- *Repairing trust if mistakes occur*

CHAPTER 9: HANDLING EMOTIONS AND CONFLICT

- *Staying calm under pressure or aggressive tactics*
- *Dealing with anger, fear, or frustration constructively*
- *Techniques for de-escalating tense situations*

CHAPTER 10: CREATIVE PROBLEM-SOLVING

- *Brainstorming fresh ideas and combining smaller solutions*
- *Seeing hidden opportunities in challenging cases*
- *Emphasizing collaboration for win-win outcomes*

CHAPTER 11: APPROACHES TO BARGAINING

- *Making the first offer vs. waiting for the other side*
- *Anchoring, concessions, and closing the gap*
- *Choosing a competitive, collaborative, or compromise style*

CHAPTER 12: UNDERSTANDING CULTURAL DIFFERENCES

- *High-context vs. low-context communication styles*
- *Respecting power distance, time views, and group focus*
- *Adapting negotiation habits for different cultural norms*

CHAPTER 13: NEGOTIATIONS IN BUSINESS

- *Contracts, salary talks, and partnership deals*
- *Researching market rates and addressing power imbalances*
- *Building long-term professional relationships*

CHAPTER 14: NEGOTIATIONS IN PERSONAL LIFE

- *Household finances, chores, and family decisions*
- *Balancing friendships and fairness in social contexts*
- *Resolving everyday conflicts through calm dialogue*

CHAPTER 15: HANDLING DIFFICULT NEGOTIATORS

- *Recognizing bullying, deception, or hostile behaviors*
- *Staying calm and setting boundaries firmly*
- *Deciding when to walk away from bad-faith talks*

CHAPTER 16: TACTICS TO AVOID

- *Why unethical tricks undermine trust*
- *Spotting misleading offers, hidden data, or empty threats*
- *Maintaining integrity and transparency*

CHAPTER 17: ETHICAL STANDARDS IN NEGOTIATION

- *Defining a moral code and protecting credibility*
- *Balancing truthfulness with strategic confidentiality*
- *Refusing unethical pressure from others*

CHAPTER 18: TECHNOLOGY AND DIGITAL NEGOTIATION

- *Using email, video calls, and online platforms effectively*
- *Cybersecurity, data privacy, and e-signatures*
- *Maintaining personal warmth in digital settings*

CHAPTER 19: CONTINUOUS IMPROVEMENT

- *Self-review, keeping a journal, and seeking feedback*
- *Avoiding plateaus and setting higher goals*
- *Learning from failures and adapting to new challenges*

CHAPTER 20: REAL-WORLD EXAMPLES AND FINAL WORDS

- *Illustrative cases from business, family, and cross-cultural deals*
- *Key takeaways to remember and apply*
- *Encouragement for ongoing growth and practice*

Chapter 1: Introduction to Negotiation Basics

Negotiation is a process where two or more sides talk about different interests or viewpoints to find an outcome that suits most, if not all, parties. When we think of negotiation, we might imagine big business deals or political agreements. But in truth, negotiation is around us every day. From asking for a better price on an item to deciding what to watch on television with a family member, these are all small forms of negotiation.

This chapter will lay out what negotiation is, why it is helpful, and what basic elements make a negotiation successful. You will learn how negotiation differs from other forms of conversation and how it fits into various parts of life. By the end, you will have a clear understanding of why negotiation is an essential skill and how it can bring about practical solutions in both simple and complex situations. We will share some "golden gems" that you can use right away. These are special tips that are not always obvious to most people.

1.1 What Is Negotiation?

Negotiation is a structured conversation where participants have something they want to achieve. Usually, each side has a goal or a set of goals. For example, you might want a higher salary from your employer, and your employer wants to keep expenses within a budget. You might want to buy a car at a lower price, and the car seller wants to make a certain profit. When both sides talk, they do not just present demands; they also share and gather information. That information helps both sides figure out what a fair agreement looks like.

A good negotiation tries to ensure that each side feels like they have gained something. This is sometimes called a "win-win" approach. However, that does not mean each side gets everything they want. Instead, it means everyone can find common ground that seems acceptable. In other cases, someone might seek a "win-lose" result where they want the other side to give up as much as possible. This style can sometimes burn bridges or lead to bad feelings, which can hurt future dealings.

1.2 Everyday Negotiations

It is a mistake to think that negotiation only happens at large conference tables or in formal settings. If you take a closer look, you might notice it in almost any conversation that involves a decision. For instance:

- **Household decisions**: Negotiating the weekly grocery budget with a partner or deciding who does which household chores.
- **Social plans**: Choosing a movie to watch with friends or picking a restaurant for dinner.
- **School or college**: Asking a teacher for a deadline extension or working on a team project where members have to divide tasks.
- **Local community**: Discussing with neighbors about property lines or shared parking spots.

In each of these situations, we use a simpler form of negotiation to find an answer that keeps everyone relatively content. Identifying these small negotiations is the first step in sharpening your skills. Once you see how often you do them, you realize the value of doing them better.

1.3 Why Negotiation Matters

Negotiation matters because it helps resolve issues without escalating conflicts. If two people cannot agree on something, a calm discussion can prevent arguments, legal disputes, or even lost relationships. Negotiation also allows both sides to share their perspectives. Sometimes, you discover that what you assumed about the other person was wrong. Gathering the right details through negotiation avoids confusion and leads to informed decisions.

A strong negotiation skill set also builds confidence. When you know how to negotiate, you do not feel powerless in situations where something is on the line. Whether it is a job offer or a family problem, you walk in with an approach to address it properly. This sense of control can reduce stress and help you focus on creative solutions.

Golden gem: A good question to ask yourself before any negotiation is, "What is the next best thing to an agreement?" This idea is sometimes called your backup plan. If you know what you will do if the negotiation fails, you have a stronger position to stand on.

1.4 Key Elements of a Negotiation

There are core elements that usually appear in most negotiations, no matter the scale. Understanding these parts can make you more aware of how to plan and respond:

1. **Interests or Goals**: Each side wants something. Goals can be financial (like price), personal (like respect), or even emotional (like recognition).
2. **Communication**: Negotiation involves an exchange of words, tone, facial expressions, and body language. If communication is poor, misunderstandings arise.
3. **Information Sharing**: Each side might share or hold back certain details. Knowing how to manage what you reveal and when you reveal it is important.
4. **Compromise or Concession**: This is when one side gives up something in exchange for something else. A balanced approach to giving and taking helps achieve an outcome that both sides can accept.
5. **Outcome or Agreement**: The final stage where both sides settle on specific terms.

Keeping these elements in mind helps you structure your approach. You might ask yourself: "What information do I need?" or "How do I guide communication to avoid confusion?" or "Which details am I okay giving up to get what I want most?"

1.5 Common Myths About Negotiation

1. **Negotiation Is Always Confrontational**: Some people think negotiations must be heated arguments. In fact, most negotiations

are calm and cooperative. Yes, there might be tension sometimes, but confrontation is not the default.
2. **It Is Just for Sales and Business**: Negotiation goes beyond money matters. It can apply to any case where people need a mutual decision.
3. **It Requires Aggression**: Some folks believe you must be very forceful to win. While assertiveness helps at times, aggression can damage trust.
4. **You Have to Be a Great Talker**: Listening is often more important than talking. Skilled negotiators know how to get the other side to share information willingly.
5. **You Must Win All Points**: In many cases, winning every single request is unrealistic. A balance of give-and-take can lead to a more lasting agreement.

Understanding these myths can help you avoid certain pitfalls. Instead of going into a discussion with fear or flawed beliefs, you can look at it as a method to solve a challenge.

1.6 Different Types of Negotiation

Not all negotiations follow the same pattern. Here are a few types you might encounter:

1. **Distributive Negotiation**: Often described as a "fixed pie" situation. For instance, if there is a single resource to split, one side's gain is the other side's loss. Examples: dividing money, splitting property, or allocating a budget among departments.
2. **Integrative Negotiation**: In these talks, both sides can find ways to increase value so everyone gains something. Instead of splitting one pie, you might look for ways to create a bigger pie. For instance, you might explore extra features or services that can be added to satisfy both sides.
3. **Multi-Party Negotiation**: More than two sides are involved. This can become complex because you have to consider multiple viewpoints and alliances. Examples include group projects, community discussions, or international treaties.

4. **Team Negotiation**: Each side might have more than one person in the room, such as a panel or a task force. Roles need to be clear to avoid confusion within your own group.

In real life, you might see a mix of these approaches. Even a family discussion can include distributive elements (like deciding how to divide chores) and integrative elements (finding creative ways to handle tasks more efficiently).

1.7 Historical Glance at Negotiation

Negotiation has existed throughout human history. Ancient traders bartered goods on trade routes, discussing prices and building relationships. Over time, societies developed rules and customs to handle conflicts and form treaties. Although the environments have changed (now we have virtual communications, for example), the core remains: people use direct discussions to settle questions about resources or power.

Throughout history, some famous talks have shaped entire regions or ended conflicts. But outside of these major events, everyday negotiations have always played a role. People have always found ways to discuss concerns and reach choices that reduce conflict. Recognizing that negotiation is not new gives you a sense of how timeless and universal these skills are.

1.8 The Impact of Negotiation on Relationships

Another reason negotiation is crucial is its effect on relationships. In families, workplaces, and communities, repeated interactions happen. If you treat every discussion as a battle that you must "win," you might risk damaging important bonds. On the other hand, a respectful style builds good will, which can help you both now and in the future.

- **Family**: Avoid turning every discussion into an argument by focusing on common interests. Over time, family members learn to trust each other more.

- **Business**: Companies often have long-term partnerships with clients and suppliers. A harsh approach might get you a short-term profit but harm your reputation.
- **Friendship**: Deciding on simple things, like how to split bills during outings, can either cause tension or build a sense of fairness.

Golden gem: Regularly reflect on how your negotiation style affects your relationships. Keep notes about how people respond to your tone or approach. Over time, you might notice patterns that you can fine-tune.

1.9 The Process of Negotiation

While no two negotiations are identical, you can outline a general process:

1. **Preparation**: You decide your goals, possible options, and your must-haves. You also research the other side's likely goals.
2. **Opening**: Each side starts by stating what they want or what they bring to the table. This sets the tone.
3. **Information Exchange**: Both sides share details, ask questions, and gather facts.
4. **Bargaining**: This is the give-and-take stage where offers and counteroffers appear.
5. **Closure**: Once an agreement is reached, it is summarized clearly. If needed, it might be put into writing.
6. **Implementation**: Each side follows the agreement.

If the sides cannot agree, they might walk away or look at different methods of resolving their issues (such as mediation or simply deciding to end the discussion). The best negotiators see these steps not as strict rules but as flexible guidelines they can adapt to each case.

1.10 Traits of an Effective Negotiator

Some traits are commonly found in good negotiators:

- **Listening Ability**: They pay close attention to what is said and what is not said. They note tone and body language.

- **Emotional Control**: Strong feelings might arise, but good negotiators keep them in check so they can think clearly.
- **Patience**: Hurrying can lead to mistakes. Giving discussions enough time to unfold often helps find better answers.
- **Clarity**: They explain their points in clear terms, so there is no guesswork about what they want or offer.
- **Problem-Solving Mindset**: Instead of only focusing on winning, they look for ways to address all main issues on the table.

It is possible to build these traits through practice, self-reflection, and occasional guidance from mentors or peers. Anyone can get better at negotiating by focusing on these basic building blocks.

1.11 Avoiding Common Pitfalls

Even with good intentions, you can make mistakes if you are not careful:

1. **Not Preparing**: Entering a negotiation without knowing what you want or what the other side might want can lead to weak positions.
2. **Being Too Rigid**: If you refuse to consider any alternative, the other side might see no reason to keep talking.
3. **Talking Too Much**: Over-sharing can reveal your weaknesses or cause confusion.
4. **Ignoring Nonverbal Cues**: Failing to notice the other side's body language might mean you miss signals of interest or discomfort.
5. **Acting Desperate**: If you show that you must close the deal at any cost, the other side might use that to push you into unfavorable terms.

By being aware of these pitfalls, you can prepare in ways that prevent them. For example, setting a clear goal or practicing your main talking points in front of a mirror can help you appear more assured.

1.12 Negotiation vs. Other Forms of Discussion

- **Negotiation vs. Debate**: A debate often has a winner and loser, where the aim is to prove a point. Negotiation seeks an outcome that satisfies both sides.
- **Negotiation vs. Persuasion**: Persuasion can be one-sided, with one person trying to change the other person's mind. In negotiation, both sides can influence each other.
- **Negotiation vs. Conflict Resolution**: Conflict resolution deals with stopping or easing intense disputes. Negotiation can be part of that process, but it can also happen in less heated cases.

Understanding these differences helps you choose the right approach. If your main goal is to find a workable solution that both sides can accept, negotiation is a better path than a debate where the goal might be to win an argument.

1.13 Early Practices to Strengthen Negotiation Skills

You do not need to wait for an important event to practice. You can start with small exercises:

1. **Price Check Exercise**: The next time you shop for something non-essential, politely ask if there is any discount or if they can include a small extra item. If they say no, that is fine. But you learn how to make a request without sounding pushy.
2. **Family Talks**: If there is a household issue—like deciding on weekly chores—suggest a small discussion. Try to understand the needs of others and see if you can propose a solution that addresses some of their concerns as well.
3. **Write Down Goals**: For a day-to-day matter, such as planning your personal budget, note what you want to achieve and what you might be willing to compromise on. This practice trains your mind to structure your approach.

These small steps build comfort with stating your position, asking the other side about theirs, and seeking ways to bridge gaps.

Golden gem: Use a notebook or an app to record small negotiations you engage in. Write down what you asked for, what the other side asked for, and the final outcome. After a while, you will see patterns in your style and can spot areas to improve.

1.14 The Role of Timing

Timing can be crucial. You might enter a negotiation too early, before you have all the details, or too late, when the other side has already made a firm choice. Knowing when to start discussions can boost your chances of success. For example, if you know a company is finalizing budgets for next year, discussing a salary raise right before that might be better than waiting until after budgets are locked.

At the same time, during the negotiation itself, some people like to rush to a conclusion while others prefer a slower pace. Matching or slightly adjusting the tempo to suit both parties can make the conversation more comfortable.

1.15 Building Confidence

A confident negotiator has an edge. Confidence does not mean arrogance; it means showing that you believe in your ability to communicate and that your requests are reasonable. Here are a few ways to build it:

1. **Prepare Thoroughly**: The more you know, the less likely you are to be caught off guard.
2. **Practice Self-Talk**: Remind yourself of your strengths and the logic behind your requests.
3. **Set Achievable Targets**: If you go in with targets that you know are too high, your confidence may drop quickly when the other side rejects them.
4. **Dress and Posture**: Even in casual settings, neat clothing and upright posture can improve how you feel about yourself, which others can sense.

Confidence is not a fixed trait. You can nurture it over time with each successful negotiation, no matter how small.

1.16 Negotiation Styles

Different people have different styles, which can sometimes be a mix:

1. **Competitive Style**: Focuses on winning, often at the expense of the other side.
2. **Collaborative Style**: Looks for shared solutions and values maintaining good relationships.
3. **Compromising Style**: Aims for a middle ground quickly, sometimes giving up more than necessary to speed up the process.
4. **Avoiding Style**: Tries to dodge conflict and might not negotiate at all unless forced.
5. **Accommodating Style**: Gives in to maintain harmony, possibly at one's own loss.

None of these styles are wrong in themselves. The context may call for one approach over another. However, being locked into one style can limit your options. Good negotiators learn to adjust styles based on the situation.

1.17 Building Trust from the Start

Before you even start discussing details, how you set the tone can affect the entire talk. Greeting the other person warmly, making friendly eye contact, or even sharing a light fact can create a more open atmosphere. Small gestures of respect—like being punctual or addressing the person properly—also build trust.

Golden gem: At the start of a negotiation, ask the other side a question about their biggest concern. This simple question can shift the focus from your own demands to them feeling heard. Then, when you make your requests, they are more likely to see you as someone who respects their perspective.

1.18 Ethical vs. Unethical Moves

In negotiations, ethics matter. Telling blatant lies can help you gain an advantage at first, but if the other side discovers the lie, your reputation and any future deals can be damaged. Even half-truths can cause complications. Some people use underhanded tricks, like hidden fees or small print in a contract. While this might work in a single negotiation, it usually hurts trust long-term.

Being ethical does not mean sharing every secret. You can keep certain facts to yourself if it is strategic to do so, but that is different from making false statements. If you are unsure if something is ethical, consider how you would feel if your method was revealed publicly.

1.19 The Link Between Negotiation and Problem-Solving

Negotiation is really just a specific type of problem-solving. You have a problem: two sides want something that might seem conflicting. Through discussion and creativity, you find a path that addresses the main needs. Many of the techniques for problem-solving—like brainstorming or using logic—apply directly to negotiation.

An example: A parent and teen might clash about curfew times. If the teen wants a midnight curfew but the parent wants 10 p.m., a purely competitive approach might end with one side forcing an outcome. But a problem-solving approach might explore the reason behind each request, such as safety, the teen's social life, and trust. They might agree on a trial period or a phone check-in system. This type of outcome might not happen if both sides are just trying to force each other.

1.20 Summary and Looking Ahead

Negotiation is a skill that touches on everyday life, big and small. You have learned about its core concepts, common myths, everyday uses, basic elements, and a glimpse of ethical considerations. You also know that strong listening, respect for the other side, and clear communication form the backbone of a good negotiation.

Moving forward, you will learn how to set clear objectives, plan effectively, communicate better, and handle tricky scenarios. In the next chapter, we will discuss how to pick your main goals, identify your limits, and map out your strategy before stepping into a negotiation. This planning step is vital, as it guides your path once the actual discussion begins.

Golden gem: Never forget that each negotiation is a chance to learn, even if it does not produce the result you wanted. By analyzing what went well and what did not, you build your skill set for the next time.

Chapter 2: Setting Clear Objectives

Before you negotiate with anyone, it is wise to know what you want and why you want it. Setting clear objectives helps you focus your energy and avoid getting sidetracked by less important details. If you have ever gone into a conversation without a clear plan, you know how easy it is to agree to something that you later regret. This chapter will guide you in deciding your key goals, creating backup plans, and keeping yourself on track once discussions start.

We will look at the reasons why goals matter, the difference between main goals and secondary needs, and how to set limits that protect your interests without causing deadlock. By the end, you will have strong techniques to clarify your intentions before stepping into a negotiation.

2.1 Why Do We Need Objectives?

An objective is a desired outcome. Having clear objectives in a negotiation is like having a roadmap. Without one, you might get lost or agree to any outcome just to end the conversation. With objectives, you can measure whether an offer is good or not.

Consider a simple example: You want to buy a laptop. If you do not set any goals, you might end up paying a higher price or accept a model that does not meet your needs. But if your objectives are to get a laptop that can handle certain programs and has a certain price range, you know exactly when to walk away from a bad deal.

Objectives also help in bigger negotiations, like job offers or partnership agreements. Knowing your salary range or the type of responsibilities you can handle will guide you. Without this clarity, you might take on tasks you dislike or accept compensation that leaves you unhappy.

2.2 Main Goals vs. Secondary Needs

Not all objectives have the same value. Some are "main goals," which are crucial for your satisfaction, while others are "secondary needs" that are nice to have but not critical. For example, if you are negotiating a salary, your main goal might be a certain monthly amount that covers your living expenses and savings. A secondary need might be extra vacation days or flexible hours. These extra points matter, but they might not be deal-breakers.

Listing out your main and secondary goals beforehand helps you see which are non-negotiable and which can be traded for something else. If you focus too much on smaller points, you risk losing the bigger prize. By keeping your eyes on what truly matters, you avoid getting distracted by side issues.

2.3 Setting Realistic Goals

It is good to aim high, but setting goals that are completely unrealistic can backfire. If the other side sees that your demands are outlandish, they might think you are not serious about reaching an agreement. For instance, if the normal market price for a product is $100, and you insist on paying only $10, the conversation might end quickly.

On the other hand, setting your goals too low might make you miss out on benefits you could have gained. Balancing these extremes requires some research. Look at common ranges, do some basic cost analysis, or ask for opinions from people with experience. By gathering facts, you can position your objectives in a range that makes sense to both you and the other side.

Golden gem: Use external sources (like market reports or official statistics) to back up your goals. When your objectives are supported by reliable information, the other side is more likely to treat them seriously.

2.4 The Importance of a Backup Plan

In negotiation circles, people often talk about a "BATNA," which stands for "Best Alternative to a Negotiated Agreement." This is a fancy way of saying "Plan B." If negotiations fall through, what is your next move? For example, if you are negotiating with one supplier, maybe you can find another supplier who might agree to the terms you want.

Having a backup plan keeps you from feeling cornered. You know that if you cannot get a good deal, you can walk away and try something else. On the flip side, if you do not have a backup plan, you might feel forced to accept a bad deal just to avoid having nothing at all.

1. **Identify Possible Alternatives**: Make a list of who else or what else can meet your needs if this negotiation fails.
2. **Compare Their Value**: Rate how good these alternatives are in terms of cost, convenience, or any measure that matters to you.
3. **Focus on Improving Your BATNA**: Sometimes, you can strengthen your backup plan, like finding more suppliers or exploring different job offers, which gives you more leverage.

2.5 Defining Walk-Away Points

A walk-away point is the moment when continuing to negotiate no longer makes sense. For example, if you want to buy a car and your budget limit is $8,000, that is your walk-away point. If the seller demands $9,000 and will not budge, you stop negotiating because the price is no longer feasible.

Clearly defining your walk-away point prevents you from making deals that harm you. It also signals to the other side that you have boundaries. If you do not have a walk-away point, you can be talked into accepting anything. Setting it beforehand ensures you keep your best interests in mind.

2.6 Methods for Organizing Objectives

1. The Checklist Method
Make a simple checklist of everything you want. Write down your main goals, secondary needs, acceptable trade-offs, and walk-away points. Review this list just before the negotiation so it is fresh in your mind.

2. The Priority Ranking Method
Assign each goal a rank. One might be "must-have," two might be "very important," three might be "moderately important," and so on. If you find yourself pressed for time, focus first on your top-ranked items.

3. The Decision Tree
A decision tree visually maps out possible negotiation paths. For example, if your request for a 10% discount is declined, you might ask for free shipping instead. If that is also declined, you might accept an extended warranty. Laying out these if-then steps helps you stay prepared.

These tools can make your objectives more concrete and help you strategize. For large negotiations with many moving parts, a well-structured plan can mean the difference between clarity and confusion.

2.7 Aligning Objectives with Personal or Organizational Values

Sometimes, your objectives might clash with your personal or organizational values. For instance, you might want to save money on a deal, but the cheapest supplier uses poor labor practices. If part of your value system is about responsible sourcing, you will have to balance saving money with moral standards.

In a corporate setting, the company might have a code of ethics. If your goal is to maximize profit by cutting corners, it might clash with that code. Aligning your objectives with these values ensures you remain consistent in what you stand for. Otherwise, you might face internal conflicts or harm your reputation.

2.8 Communicating Your Objectives Clearly

Once you have set your goals, how you communicate them matters. You do not necessarily have to reveal every detail to the other side. Telling them your walk-away point could put you at a disadvantage, for example. But you do want to make sure they understand your main positions so they can respond effectively.

To communicate well:

1. **State Intentions Early**: Without giving away all details, let the other side know the broad outcome you are aiming for.
2. **Use Plain Language**: Avoid confusing terms. People trust you more if you speak in a straightforward way.
3. **Check for Understanding**: Ask if they see where you are coming from. This can prevent simple misunderstandings from turning into bigger issues.

2.9 Staying Open to Adjustments

While objectives are important, staying rigid can shut down potentially good outcomes. If the other side offers something that is different from what you asked for but still meets your needs, consider it. For example, if you wanted an 8% pay increase but instead they offer extra benefits that are valuable to you, it might still be worth it.

It is wise to balance clarity in your aims with some flexibility. Negotiation is a dynamic process. Your partner might suggest creative solutions you had not considered. If you cling too closely to a specific approach, you might miss better opportunities.

Golden gem: Remember that sometimes the other side's proposal could solve a problem you did not even realize you had. Keep an open mind and weigh the total value of an offer rather than focusing only on one component.

2.10 The Role of Research in Setting Objectives

Quality research can help you set objectives that are both fair and feasible:

1. **Market Analysis**: If you are in a commercial setting, check the usual market prices.
2. **Legal Guidelines**: For certain contracts or agreements, laws might dictate minimum standards or rights.
3. **Expert Opinions**: If it is a technical deal, consult with someone who understands the ins and outs.
4. **Past Deals**: Look at your own history or others' histories for patterns of what worked and what did not.

By comparing the information you gather, you form an objective that is grounded in reality. This makes it harder for the other side to dismiss your requests as baseless. It also gives you talking points to defend your position.

2.11 Combining Multiple Goals into One Strategy

Sometimes, you do not have just one goal. You might want a certain price plus a certain delivery schedule plus certain quality standards. Trying to negotiate each piece separately could be confusing. Instead, you might want to combine them into one proposal.

For instance: "We will pay a bit higher if you can deliver the product sooner and guarantee a higher standard." This lets you address multiple objectives in a single statement. The other side might be more open to this because you are showing flexibility. You are not just demanding a lower price; you are offering something in exchange (like a slightly higher payment) to get what you want in terms of time and quality.

2.12 Pitfalls in Objective-Setting

1. **Setting Vague Goals**: For example, saying "I want a good deal" does not help much. Be specific: "I want a 10% reduction or free shipping."

2. **Overlooking the Other Side's Needs**: If your goals ignore their needs entirely, you might reach an impasse.
3. **Failing to Update Goals Mid-Negotiation**: Sometimes you learn new facts halfway through. Sticking to outdated objectives can harm your final outcome.
4. **Letting Emotions Cloud Judgement**: You might be offended by something the other side says, causing you to set overly harsh objectives or refuse to budge.

Being aware of these traps helps you avoid them. Clear, flexible, and properly researched objectives stand a higher chance of leading to a successful agreement.

2.13 Working with a Team on Objectives

When negotiating as part of a team, setting objectives can be more complex. Different people might prioritize different things. One teammate might care about budget, another about time, and another about long-term partnership. If you do not align these internal goals, you risk undermining your own side.

Steps to align team objectives:

1. **Internal Discussion**: Before meeting the other side, hold a meeting with your team.
2. **Rank Each Person's Priorities**: Find out where everyone stands.
3. **Combine and Refine**: Create a shared list of main goals, secondary needs, and walk-away points that the entire team supports.
4. **Assign Roles**: Decide who will speak about which topics, and who will handle clarifications.

By doing this, you avoid confusion during the actual negotiation. Everyone knows the plan, and you come across as more united and clear.

2.14 Setting Goals for Personal Negotiations

Negotiation is not always about professional deals. Personal talks matter too, like deciding household budgets or planning a vacation. You still need clear goals. For example, in planning a vacation with your family, your main goal might be to keep total expenses under a certain amount, while a secondary goal might be to find a place with child-friendly activities.

In personal settings, emotions can run high because you are dealing with close people. Stating your goals calmly and logically helps keep the talk on track. It also shows respect for others' needs. If you know your partner's main concern is a restful location, you can look for a destination that fits your budget and still offers the peace they want.

2.15 Documenting Objectives

It is helpful to put your objectives in writing, even if just for yourself. Documentation makes your goals tangible. You can review them to ensure they make sense, add new points if something comes to mind, and remove points that no longer matter.

In bigger negotiations, you might use shared documents so your teammates can see and comment on them. This helps everyone stay on the same page. During the actual negotiation, having a reference can keep you from forgetting important items.

2.16 Examples of Clear Objective-Setting

1. **Job Offer Scenario**
   - **Main Goal**: Salary of at least $50,000 per year.
   - **Secondary Needs**: Health benefits, flexible work hours, professional development funding.
   - **Walk-Away**: Less than $45,000 with no benefits.
2. **Event Planning with a Venue**
   - **Main Goal**: A total cost under $5,000 for the event.
   - **Secondary Needs**: Option to have a projector and a stage included.

- **Walk-Away**: Any package over $6,000 without the requested extras.
3. **Family Car Purchase**
    - **Main Goal**: Buy a reliable car within $8,000.
    - **Secondary Needs**: Good gas mileage, decent resale value.
    - **Walk-Away**: If the seller refuses to provide service history or if the total cost goes above $9,000.

By laying out these points, you know exactly when the deal meets your needs and when you must step away.

2.17 Handling Shifting Objectives

Sometimes, as a negotiation progresses, you or the other side discover new details. Your shipping requirement might not be as urgent as you thought, or the other side might realize they can offer a better price. This new information can change goals mid-way.

You should not treat your objectives as carved in stone. While you should remain firm about your key interests, be open to modifying certain elements if it helps close a more favorable deal overall. Just make sure to assess changes logically instead of on a whim.

Golden gem: If a new fact surfaces, take a brief pause to discuss it with your team or to think alone. Rushing to adjust your goals without thought can lead to decisions you regret later.

2.18 Communicating Goals to the Other Side

Deciding how much of your plan to reveal is an art. If you reveal everything—including your absolute walk-away points—they might push you right to that limit. If you share too little, they might think you are not negotiating in good faith.

A balanced approach might be:

- Share your primary aim in broad terms.
- Keep your exact walk-away figure private.

- Offer glimpses of your secondary needs so they know there is room for trade-offs.

For instance, you could say, "Our main interest is securing a fair long-term contract that benefits both sides. We also have concerns about timely delivery, so that is a big factor for us." This statement reveals some priorities without giving away all your cards.

2.19 Strategy vs. Tactics

In negotiation, a **strategy** is your overall plan, which includes your objectives, your walk-away points, and the type of relationship you want to build. **Tactics** are the specific actions or moves you use during the negotiation, such as making the first offer or waiting for the other side to speak. When you have clear objectives, your tactics become easier to define. For example, if your main goal is to secure a certain price range, a common tactic might be to make the first offer so you can "anchor" the discussion on your target.

2.20 Conclusion and Next Steps

Objectives are the foundation of a strong negotiation. By knowing what you truly want, what you can compromise on, and when to walk away, you step into discussions with clarity. You also avoid the chaos of decisions made on the fly, which often leads to poor results. Clear objectives let you judge any proposal that comes your way. You can quickly tell if it meets your needs or if you should counter-offer.

In the next chapters, we will look at how to gather information, prepare thoroughly, and communicate effectively. Your objectives will form the backbone of these actions. Everything from how you speak to the other side to the research you do will be guided by the clear goals you set. Continue to develop these skills, and you will find that your negotiations become more structured and less stressful.

Golden gem: Even if you do not walk away with your perfect outcome, having clear objectives allows you to measure what you got against what you needed. This measurement helps you learn and adjust for future negotiations, making each experience a stepping stone to greater skill.

Chapter 3: Research and Information Gathering

Research and information gathering form the backbone of any negotiation. Without accurate facts, you risk relying on guesses or assumptions. The purpose of this chapter is to explain how and where to look for useful data, what kinds of information can help you, and how to organize that information. When you show the other side that you know your facts, you increase your credibility. This, in turn, gives you greater confidence when you present your offers or counteroffers.

We will look at different ways to collect details, such as using the internet, talking to experts, or examining past deals. We will also discuss common mistakes people make in their research. By the end of this chapter, you should have a clear plan for how to start gathering the information you need before stepping into any negotiation. This information will guide your decisions on what to ask for and what to accept.

3.1 Why Research Matters

Accurate information prevents you from entering a negotiation blindly. Think of the difference between trying to solve a puzzle with a clear picture in front of you versus trying to piece it together from memory. When you have facts on hand, you can make logical requests and understand if the other side is being fair or not.

Research also helps you find hidden opportunities. You might spot a special tax incentive that could help lower costs, or discover that the other side has a new product line they want to promote. Such details let you propose ideas that fit both sides' interests.

Golden gem: Sometimes, the other side may not even be aware of all the facts you bring. By presenting new information, you can shape the discussion in a productive way.

3.2 Types of Information to Collect

It can be helpful to think of the information you need in different categories. Not all data will matter for every negotiation, but having a list of categories prevents you from overlooking something crucial.

1. **Market Data**
    - **Pricing Trends**: Know the typical price range for a product or service.
    - **Supply and Demand**: If demand is high and supply is low, the price may be driven up. If demand is low, it may give you a chance to negotiate a cheaper deal.
    - **Competitor Information**: Are there other sellers or buyers that might offer a better deal?
2. **Cost Details**
    - **Production Costs**: If you understand the cost to produce an item, you can gauge how much profit margin the other side might have.
    - **Overhead and Operating Expenses**: In a business negotiation, it helps to know what expenses each side handles and how flexible they are.
3. **Legal or Regulatory Factors**
    - **Local Laws**: Some places have rules about minimum wages, safety standards, or consumer protection.
    - **Industry Regulations**: For certain fields like finance or healthcare, extra guidelines could affect the terms of any deal.
4. **Background on the Other Party**
    - **Past Deals**: If they have a track record of making deals under certain terms, that might indicate their usual range.
    - **Company Culture**: Some organizations emphasize long-term relationships, while others focus mainly on price.
    - **Financial Status**: Are they thriving, or are they in a tough spot? This can affect how much they need a deal.
5. **Your Own Resources and Needs**
    - **Budget Limits**: Know exactly how much you can spend or what you can offer.

- **Time Constraints**: If you have a tight timeline, your negotiating power may differ from when you have no deadline.
- **Alternative Options**: If you have several choices, you can negotiate from a stronger position.

3.3 Where to Find Information

Now that we have outlined the types of information to collect, the next step is learning where to find these details. Some sources are simple, while others require a little creativity.

1. **Public Records and Databases**
   - Government websites often publish reports on pricing, trends, or guidelines.
   - Libraries and online databases can provide market analyses.
   - Industry associations sometimes produce free or low-cost reports.
2. **News Outlets and Trade Journals**
   - Local or international newspapers might report on industry changes that can affect negotiations.
   - Trade journals often give in-depth coverage of trends and success stories in a particular field.
   - Business magazines can highlight emerging market conditions.
3. **Online Research**
   - Company websites often list their products, services, and even financial statements.
   - Professional networking sites can show you the background of key decision-makers.
   - Customer reviews or social media might reveal what the public thinks about a company's brand or practices.
4. **Direct Interaction**
   - **Interviews or Surveys**: Talking to people in the same industry can give you insights into common terms or prices.
   - **Events and Conferences**: Seminars and workshops let you network, learn from experts, and gather real-world stories.

- **Cold Calls or Email**: Sometimes, you can reach out directly to a potential partner or competitor to ask for basic data.
5. **Past Documents and Records**
    - If you have negotiated with the same party before, check your files to see what was agreed upon.
    - Look at your own past negotiations, even if they involved different parties, to identify patterns.

3.4 Organizing the Information

Collecting data is only part of the task. You also need a way to store and sort it so you can use it during the negotiation. You might choose a digital spreadsheet, a folder of printed materials, or a research app. The key is to make sure you can quickly find what you need.

- **Categorize by Topic**: Use headings like "Price Data," "Legal Requirements," or "Competition."
- **Prioritize**: Label or highlight the most important data points so you do not get lost in less relevant details.
- **Keep a Summary**: After collecting your main facts, write a one-page summary that highlights the key items. That way, if you do not have time to look through everything, you can still recall the main points.

Golden gem: Some negotiators create "cheat sheets" of their best data. These might include quick stats, relevant laws, and bullet points that support their offers.

3.5 Validating Your Sources

Not all information is created equal. Some websites or reports may be out of date or biased. Make sure to cross-check facts from multiple sources. If you find conflicting data, decide which source you trust more based on reputation or date of publication.

Also, try to confirm if the data you are using is still relevant. Markets can change quickly. A price range from last year might be entirely different now, especially if there has been a major shift in demand.

3.6 Using Expert Opinions

Expert opinions can make your negotiation stance much stronger. If you are negotiating about technology systems, an IT specialist can help you understand the real cost and benefits. If you are dealing with property, a real estate agent's view might help you see hidden issues or advantages.

When you bring an expert into the negotiation, clarify their role. Are they there just to advise you privately, or to speak on your behalf? Experts who speak during the discussion can add credibility, but you must make sure they are able to communicate clearly. An expert who uses confusing language might make the other side suspicious or bored.

3.7 Respecting Confidential Information

Sometimes, you might come across confidential data, like a company's internal cost structure or a competitor's planned launch date. Be careful about how you handle such data. Using information you obtained in a suspicious way can backfire. The other side might lose trust in you if they think you obtained or used sensitive details through improper methods.

In certain negotiations, a non-disclosure agreement (NDA) might be in place to protect both parties. Make sure you follow any rules about what you can or cannot share. An ethical approach to information gathering and usage helps you maintain a good reputation and can foster a more respectful discussion.

3.8 Using Research to Understand the Other Side's Interests

Your goal is not just to gather numbers and facts about the item or service. You also want to learn about the other side's priorities. For instance, if the other side's main concern is speed of delivery, you might focus your research on how you can meet or beat their timeline. If they care mostly about cost, you might look for ways to reduce expenses so you can propose a lower price.

Try to think like the other side. Ask questions such as:

- What challenges are they facing right now?
- What benefits might they gain if they partner with me?
- Are they looking for a quick sale or a long-term partnership?

Answers to these questions can help you shape your offers so that they feel more attractive. You can also anticipate objections. If you realize that your timeline might not meet their immediate needs, you can prepare ways to speed up the process or offer a partial delivery earlier.

3.9 Avoiding Analysis Paralysis

Sometimes people get stuck researching and never move forward. This is called "analysis paralysis." While it is important to be well-informed, you do not want to delay your negotiation endlessly just to gather a bit more data. Set a reasonable time limit for your research phase.

You can also decide on the specific items you need to find and stop once you have those details. If you discover something new during the negotiation, you can always do some quick follow-up research. But do not let the fear of missing data stop you from taking action.

Golden gem: A good rule of thumb is to gather the "vital few" pieces of information. Focus on the 20% of data that will handle 80% of your concerns.

3.10 How Much Information Should You Reveal?

Having a lot of data is valuable, but how much do you share with the other side? Revealing certain facts, like your own budget limit, might weaken your position. On the other hand, showing that you have done solid research can make the other side treat you more seriously.

A balanced approach is:

1. **Reveal Information That Builds Trust**: If you find a relevant market study that supports a fair price range, you can share it. This shows you are not just guessing.
2. **Protect Key Details**: Financial limits, specific pain points, or urgent timelines may be best kept to yourself unless there is a strategic benefit to sharing them.
3. **Use Data to Make Logical Arguments**: Refer to your research as reasons why your offer or counteroffer is sensible.

3.11 Conducting a Pre-Negotiation Meeting

If you are negotiating with a team, consider a short meeting to discuss the key research findings before the actual negotiation. Each team member can present their area of expertise. One might have looked at market prices, another at legal matters, and another at the other side's background. By consolidating this information, you form a unified plan.

During the pre-meeting, decide who will speak about each topic. For instance, if you have a colleague who understands the technical side, let them answer any questions that arise on that front. This prevents confusion during the actual discussion.

3.12 Field Research and Observation

Not all research needs to be done online or through documents. Field research can sometimes reveal insights you would never find in a report.

For example, if you are negotiating with a local restaurant to host an event, visit the restaurant during a busy time to see how they handle crowds. That might give you a clue about their capacity or their service quality.

- **Mystery Shopping**: Pretend to be a regular customer to see how they treat clients.
- **Surveys and Feedback**: If relevant, gather opinions from people who have used the product or service you will discuss.
- **On-Site Observation**: Observe how the other side operates. Do they seem organized or chaotic?

This hands-on approach can sometimes provide golden pieces of data that a formal report would never mention.

3.13 Handling Conflicting Information

It is common to find conflicting data. One source might say the average market rate is $500, while another claims it is $600. If you do not sort this out, you could end up confused and unable to argue convincingly.

1. **Evaluate Sources**: Decide which source is more likely to be reliable. A government or well-known industry association might be more accurate than an unknown blog.
2. **Look at Dates**: Market rates from three years ago may no longer apply. Pick the most current data.
3. **Use Averages or Ranges**: Sometimes, it helps to present a range, like "Market rates appear to fall between $500 and $600." This gives you flexibility during discussions.

3.14 Understanding Cultural and Social Factors

If your negotiation crosses cultural or social boundaries, it is wise to learn about norms that might affect how the other side reacts. For example, some cultures value formal greetings or place importance on certain words. Others might expect a round of small talk before discussing business.

Even within the same culture, different age groups or regional groups might have their own communication style. If you are not prepared, you might accidentally offend the other side or fail to notice when they are showing signs of discomfort.

3.15 Testing Assumptions Through Small Questions

Before you get deep into big demands, you can test your assumptions by asking small, low-risk questions. For instance, if you think the other side is concerned about speed, you might casually ask, "How soon would you like to see this project completed?" Their answer might confirm your assumption or show you that timeline is not their main worry.

These small questions work like a pilot test. If you find that your assumption was wrong, you can adjust your approach before making a larger offer or request.

3.16 The Role of Data in Building Your Argument

Once you have gathered information, think about how to structure it into a clear, logical argument. The simplest way is to present a fact and explain how it supports your position. For example, "According to Market Report X, the standard rate for this service ranges from $100 to $150 per hour. We propose paying $120 per hour, which is well within the normal range."

This method makes it harder for the other side to dismiss your offer as random or unfair. They might counter with their own data, which can lead to a discussion about which numbers are most reliable. But either way, you are talking about facts, not just opinions.

3.17 Learning from Past Mistakes

If you have negotiated before and things went wrong, analyze what happened. Did you fail to check market rates? Did you not know the other side's main concern? Use this as a lesson for future research. It might mean you need to start your fact-finding process earlier, double-check certain figures, or consult different experts.

Golden gem: Keep a short log of each negotiation's research steps. Write down what worked, what did not, and how you might improve next time. Over multiple negotiations, you will build a personalized guide to researching effectively.

3.18 Online Tools and Software

These days, there are many online tools that can make research easier:

- **Price Comparison Websites**: Great for product-based negotiations.
- **Social Media Listening**: If the other side is active on social platforms, you can see how they engage with customers or if they post updates about new projects.
- **Data Analysis Software**: If you have a large amount of data, software can help you spot trends or patterns.

However, be mindful that not every tool is accurate or unbiased. Spend some time verifying any data you get, especially if it comes from a free or unfamiliar site.

3.19 Ethical Considerations in Research

While collecting facts is important, you should do it in an ethical way. Spying on the other side, hacking emails, or misrepresenting yourself to gain sensitive details crosses the line. Even if you come across that data by accident, using it might harm your reputation or lead to legal trouble.

Stick to legal and fair methods of information gathering. If you happen to find private details, consider whether using them is worth the risk. In most cases, a fair negotiation rests on open, honest data that both sides can reasonably access.

3.20 Putting It All Together

When you have done thorough research, you will notice a difference in your negotiation conversations. You will feel more assured, speak with clarity, and know when to push back against offers that seem unrealistic.

Imagine you are negotiating with a client who wants you to deliver a complex project in half the normal time for a regular price. Because of your research, you can say, "I checked with several contractors and industry guidelines. They show that reducing the timeline by 50% can raise costs by about 30%. We want to meet your timeline, but we must adjust the price to cover extra resources."

By referencing verifiable data, you shift the conversation from a debate about your opinion to a professional talk grounded in facts. That can help you both reach an agreement that makes sense.

Conclusion

Research and information gathering provide a strong base for any negotiation. By knowing market norms, understanding the other side's likely viewpoint, and having data ready to back up your offers, you go into talks with an advantage. Avoid the common pitfalls of collecting too much data or relying on dubious sources. Instead, aim for quality over quantity. Confirm your facts, organize them for easy access, and use them ethically.

In the next chapter, we will look at Preparation Tools and Techniques. We will see how to turn your research into a practical plan. This includes setting up checklists, role-playing, and other methods that help you enter the negotiation room with confidence.

Golden gem: The difference between an amateur negotiator and a seasoned one often comes down to good research. Solid facts not only strengthen your case but also help you see the real situation clearly, leading to wiser decisions.

Chapter 4: Preparation Tools and Techniques

Preparation goes hand in hand with research. Once you have your facts, you need a plan for how to use them. Think of preparation as putting your research into a framework that guides your actions during the negotiation. This chapter will show you various tools and techniques that help you become more organized and confident.

We will cover checklists, mock sessions, mental rehearsals, and other methods that ensure you do not walk into the negotiation unprepared. Even simple actions like mapping out your first few sentences or preparing your documents in order can make a big difference in the final outcome. By the end of this chapter, you will know how to create a plan that draws from your research and sets you up for a successful discussion.

4.1 Making a Negotiation Checklist

A negotiation checklist is an easy but powerful tool. It serves as a reminder of what you need before, during, and after the talk. Think of it like a packing list for a trip. If you skip something important, you might not realize it until it is too late.

What to Include on Your Checklist:

1. **Key Objectives**: State your main and secondary goals clearly.
2. **Supporting Facts**: List the key data points from your research that support each goal.
3. **Possible Offers and Concessions**: Decide what you can offer if the other side requests a compromise.
4. **Walk-Away Points**: Note the minimum or maximum limits you will accept.
5. **Documents Needed**: Contracts, cost estimates, product samples, or whatever is relevant.
6. **Contact Information**: Make sure you have the names and numbers of the people involved, in case something comes up.

This checklist keeps you focused. During a busy or stressful moment in the negotiation, you can glance at it to confirm you are on track. You can also tick off items as you address them, avoiding confusion about what has been discussed and what remains.

4.2 Role-Playing or Mock Negotiations

A mock negotiation is a practice session. You can invite a friend, family member, or colleague to play the role of the other side. Provide them with a short brief about the situation so they can respond as realistically as possible. Then, go through a simulated negotiation.

Benefits of Role-Playing:

- **Identify Gaps**: You might realize you have no solid response to a specific question.
- **Build Confidence**: Rehearsing your main talking points helps you feel more at ease.
- **Get Objective Feedback**: The person playing the other side can tell you if your arguments make sense or if your body language seems nervous.

If you are part of a team, a mock session can ensure everyone understands their role. Maybe one team member is responsible for financial details, another for technical specs, and another for final approval. Rehearsing helps you avoid talking over each other or missing points.

Golden gem: Ask the person playing the other side to be a bit tougher than you expect the real party to be. That way, the actual negotiation will feel easier by comparison.

4.3 Mental Rehearsal

Not everyone has time to do a full role-play. In that case, you can perform a mental rehearsal. Close your eyes and imagine the entire negotiation step by step. Picture where you will sit, how you will greet the other side, and what your first statements will be. Then, visualize possible questions or objections they might raise. Think about how you will respond calmly and confidently.

This mental exercise helps reduce anxiety and prepares your brain to handle surprises. Athletes often use visualization techniques to see themselves performing well. In the same way, seeing yourself handle a negotiation effectively can enhance your actual performance.

4.4 Deciding on the Meeting Format and Location

Sometimes you have control over where and how the negotiation will take place. Other times, you do not. If you do have a choice, consider these points:

- **Location**: A neutral venue (like a meeting room not owned by either party) can make both sides feel on equal footing.
- **Timing**: Pick a time that allows both sides to be relaxed and not rushed. Avoid scheduling right before a major holiday or late on a Friday when people are tired.
- **Online vs. In-Person**: Video calls can save travel time, but in-person meetings allow for better reading of body language.
- **Seating Arrangement**: In some cases, sitting side by side (instead of across a table) can promote a sense of collaboration.

These details might seem minor, but they can impact the mood of the negotiation. A crowded, noisy cafe is not the best place for sensitive topics. A well-lit, quiet conference room can create a more focused atmosphere.

4.5 Planning Your Opening Statement

The first things you say can shape the entire talk. If you come across as aggressive, the other side might become defensive. If you seem too timid, they might think they can push you around. Planning your opening statement ensures you strike the right tone.

Ideas for an Effective Opening:

- **Friendly Greeting**: A simple hello and a polite comment about the meeting format or the day can break the ice.
- **Clear Purpose**: State why you are meeting: "I'm glad we can discuss how we might work together on this project."
- **Positive Tone**: Even if you have tough demands, you can start by acknowledging the other side's time or expertise.
- **Outline the Agenda**: If it is a formal session, mention the points you want to cover, so everyone knows what to expect.

4.6 Having a Strategy for Questions

Questions can guide the direction of the conversation. Good negotiators often ask more questions than they answer. This helps them gather information, clarify details, and understand the other side's position.

- **Open-Ended Questions**: "What are your thoughts on extending the deadline?" encourages a detailed response.
- **Closed-Ended Questions**: "Do you agree with the proposed budget?" can force a yes/no answer, useful for quick checks.
- **Follow-Up Questions**: "Can you explain how you arrived at that figure?" can uncover the reason behind a statement.

Plan a list of questions in advance. Arrange them from the most important to the least. During the actual talk, you might not use all, but having them ready ensures you never get stuck.

4.7 Using Visual Aids and Handouts

In more complex negotiations, charts, graphs, or slides can be a big help. For instance, if you are discussing costs that vary month to month, a simple chart showing the fluctuation can clarify your point. If you are proposing a timeline for a project, a color-coded schedule can illustrate when each phase will happen.

When you give someone a visual aid or handout, they can review it on their own time. This reduces the chance of misunderstandings. It also shows you have done your homework, which can boost your credibility.

4.8 Planning for Potential Outcomes

Sometimes the other side might say "no" to your main proposal. What is your next move? This is where contingency plans come in. If you cannot agree on one aspect, can you shift the discussion to another angle? For example, if they refuse a price cut, can you ask for free shipping or a longer payment period?

Make a chart or list of the potential outcomes and how you will respond. Consider the best-case scenario, the worst-case scenario, and several in between. This mental preparation keeps you from feeling stuck if the deal moves in an unexpected direction.

Golden gem: Think through "if-they-say-this, I-will-do-that" scenarios. That way, you are not scrambling for solutions on the spot.

4.9 Coordinating with a Team

If you are not negotiating alone, it is vital to decide who does what. Some roles you might have in a team negotiation include:

- **Lead Spokesperson**: This person does the main talking and states the team's position.
- **Note-Taker**: Someone should record key points, offers, and agreements.
- **Subject Expert**: A person who handles specific questions about costs, technology, or legalities.
- **Observer**: Sometimes, a quiet observer watches body language and mood in the room.

Before the negotiation, hold a meeting so each member knows their role. This reduces confusion and prevents your side from accidentally contradicting each other. If a topic arises that relates to a certain member's expertise, the lead can hand the conversation over to them.

4.10 Time Management

Negotiations can drag on, especially if complex details arise. Planning how much time you can spend helps you keep control. You might decide that if you cannot reach an agreement within two hours, you will schedule another session or reconsider your approach. You can even set mini-deadlines for certain segments. For example, "We will spend the first 30 minutes discussing budget and the next 30 on timelines."

Effective time management also shows respect for everyone's schedule. If the other side sees that you are organized and not wasting time, they may respond better to your proposals.

4.11 Physical and Mental Readiness

Many people overlook the need to be physically and mentally ready. A good night's sleep can make a difference in how sharp you are. Light exercise or a short walk can reduce stress, while heavy meals might slow you down. If you are feeling anxious, consider simple breathing exercises to calm your nerves.

- **Eat and Hydrate**: You do not want to feel lightheaded or distracted.
- **Dress Appropriately**: Wear clothes that match the setting but are also comfortable enough for a potentially long discussion.
- **Have a Clear Mind**: Avoid rushing from another stressful activity. Give yourself a bit of time to refocus.

4.12 Deciding Whether to Make the First Offer

One debate in negotiation strategy is whether you should open with an offer or let the other side do so. Opening first can help "anchor" the discussion around your figures or terms. However, if you do not have enough information, making the first offer might backfire.

Consider these factors before deciding:

- **Confidence in Your Data**: If you have solid research showing a fair range, you can open.
- **Experience and Position**: If you are new or uncertain, waiting might let you gauge the other side's stance first.
- **Competition or Urgency**: In certain markets, if you do not make a strong initial offer, the other side might go elsewhere.

Think about these points while preparing, and discuss with your team if you have one. You might also prepare a backup plan in case the other side makes an unreasonable first offer.

4.13 Drafting a Possible Agreement

In some negotiations, it is useful to have a draft contract or agreement ready. This draft is not final, but it gives a structure the other side can respond to. You can fill in the blanks with the terms you want. They can suggest changes, and you can negotiate from that starting point.

A draft can save time, especially if the deal involves legal or detailed terms. However, be sure to mention that it is only a draft. Otherwise, the other side might feel you are forcing them into a fixed contract.

4.14 Reviewing Past Negotiations

Before your next negotiation, review any notes or contracts from similar past experiences. What were the sticking points? How were they resolved? Did you notice any patterns in how your counterpart approached the discussion?

By reflecting on these experiences, you can avoid repeating mistakes. You can also identify strengths in your past approach that you can use again. If you keep a log or journal of your negotiations, this becomes easier to track over time.

4.15 Testing Your Equipment and Materials

If you plan to use slides or online tools, test them beforehand. Make sure your computer, projector, or internet connection works properly. A technical glitch can break the flow of the negotiation. If you are sharing documents or screens online, practice opening and presenting them to ensure no awkward delays.

Similarly, organize any printed documents or business cards in a neat folder. Scrambling through papers looks unprofessional and can make the other side doubt your readiness.

4.16 Preparing Emotionally

Negotiations can be tense. You may feel pressure to get a certain outcome, and the other side might bring demands that upset you. Emotional preparation is as important as any checklist or role-play. Some steps:

1. **Identify Your Own Triggers**: If certain topics upset you, plan a calm response.
2. **Use Neutral Language**: Mentally rehearse polite phrases that can lower tension, such as "I see your point" or "Let's see how we can address that."
3. **Plan for Breaks**: It is okay to suggest a short pause if things get heated.
4. **Stay Positive**: A solution-based mindset helps you see obstacles as challenges to overcome rather than personal attacks.

4.17 Anticipating the Other Side's Tactics

Preparation also means guessing what tricks or methods the other side might use. Could they try to stall? Will they bring up past deals to anchor the price? Are they likely to make a false final offer to see if you will fold?

While you cannot predict everything, having a general sense of possible tactics helps you avoid surprises. You can even practice responding to them in your mock sessions or mental rehearsals. For example, if they present a very low first offer, you can calmly respond with data supporting your counteroffer.

4.18 Gathering Support or Allies

In some cases, you might benefit from outside support. For instance, if you are negotiating a lease for a property, you might bring a property lawyer. If you are talking about technical products, a consultant might lend credibility. Having someone by your side who can back up your points can make you feel more secure.

However, be careful not to overwhelm the other side with too many people or advisors. Sometimes, too large a group can feel intimidating and may slow down the process. Decide how many people are truly necessary for an effective session.

4.19 Final Review Before the Negotiation

On the day or evening before, do a final review:

1. **Check Your Documents**: Make sure everything is up to date and printed if needed.
2. **Revisit Your Main Objectives**: Keep them fresh in your mind.
3. **Recall Key Data Points**: Be ready to cite them if asked.
4. **Prepare Mentally**: Take a moment to relax and gather your thoughts.

Doing this final run-through helps you catch last-minute errors or changes. You enter the negotiation with clarity, not scrambling at the last moment.

4.20 Summary and Next Steps

Preparation tools and techniques give you a structured approach to handle negotiations. Whether you use checklists, role-play, mental rehearsals, or detailed agendas, the aim is the same: to ensure you walk into the discussion ready to tackle questions, counteroffers, and challenges. Proper preparation also keeps you calm, making it easier to find creative solutions on the spot.

In the chapters ahead, we will discuss communication fundamentals, active listening, and body language. These topics will help you use your preparation effectively. After all, having a well-thought plan is good, but knowing how to deliver your points and read the other side's signals can make the difference between a stalled talk and a successful deal.

Golden gem: Remember that thorough preparation shows respect for both your own time and the other side's. It signals that you take the negotiation seriously, which can set a positive tone from the start.

Chapter 5: Communication Fundamentals

Communication is the core of any negotiation. Even if you have solid facts and a strong plan, you still need clear and effective communication to share your ideas and understand the other person's viewpoints. This chapter looks at the basics of communication, including word choice, tone, clarity, and methods of expressing ideas. We will also discuss how to handle different communication styles, manage disagreements, and keep the conversation moving toward a solution.

We will explore how to speak in a simple, direct way without causing confusion. We will see why it is important to choose our words carefully and pay attention to nonverbal signals, even though we will go deeper into nonverbal aspects in Chapter 7. By the end of this chapter, you should be able to express your position confidently and respond to the other side in a way that improves understanding rather than creating tension.

5.1 The Meaning of Communication in Negotiations

Communication is not just talking. It involves sending and receiving messages in different forms. During a negotiation, communication includes your spoken words, your tone of voice, and even your pauses. If your communication is unclear, the other person might misunderstand your position or think you are not sincere. If your communication is overly complicated, you risk losing their attention.

Key points in negotiation communication:

1. **Clarity**: Use direct words rather than vague phrases.
2. **Purpose**: Every statement should support a goal.
3. **Responsiveness**: React to what the other side says, showing that you are listening.
4. **Control of Emotions**: Even if you feel upset, try to maintain a calm style.

Communication matters because it affects how the other person sees you. If they feel you speak in a confusing or aggressive way, they might close off or become defensive. On the other hand, if you speak clearly and politely, they might trust you more.

5.2 Elements of Clear Language

Clear language is a skill. It means choosing words and sentence structures that others can easily follow. If you use long, winding sentences, or if you fill your speech with too many technical terms, people may not catch your main point. In negotiations, that can lead to wrong assumptions or wasted time.

- **Short Sentences**: Fewer words per sentence helps people keep up with you.
- **Common Vocabulary**: Use everyday words rather than industry jargon, unless you are certain the other side knows those terms.
- **Logical Flow**: Arrange your statements in a sequence that makes sense. For example, you can start with your goal, then offer facts that support it, then wrap up with a summary of what you want from them.

Clear language also reduces the risk of being misunderstood. In a sensitive business deal, a single confusing phrase can spark tension. It is better to be brief and explicit about what you need, what you offer, and why it matters.

5.3 Tone of Voice and Pacing

Even if your words are well-chosen, your tone of voice can change how those words are heard. A sarcastic or harsh tone might offend the other side, even if your actual request is reasonable. A soft, calm tone can help them see you as cooperative, even if you are asking for a big concession.

1. **Volume**: Talking too loudly can seem aggressive. Talking too quietly might show a lack of confidence.
2. **Pitch**: A steady pitch conveys control. A highly variable pitch might be seen as nervousness.

3. **Pace**: If you speak too fast, they might miss details. If you speak too slowly, they might lose patience.

Aim for a tone that is friendly yet firm. Practice slowing down slightly if you tend to rush through important points. When you reach a key statement—like your main request—pause briefly beforehand so the other side knows something important is coming. That pause can make them pay closer attention.

5.4 Choosing the Right Words to Avoid Tension

Certain words can trigger a negative reaction. For example, if you say, "You must do this," it might sound commanding. If you say, "Can we find a way to achieve this together?" it sounds more cooperative. Be mindful of how the other person might feel when they hear your words. Instead of sounding like you are giving orders, phrase your requests in a way that shows mutual respect.

You can also reduce tension by focusing on facts, not personal judgments. Compare these two statements:

- **Judgment**: "You set an unreasonable price."
- **Fact-Focused**: "According to three local listings, the usual rate is about 15% lower."

The second statement points to data rather than insulting the other side. This approach encourages them to respond with their own facts rather than reacting to an accusation. By staying fact-focused, you keep the conversation on the problem, not on personal attacks.

5.5 Emotional Intelligence in Communication

Emotional intelligence means being aware of your own feelings, understanding how others might feel, and using that awareness to guide your words. During a negotiation, tempers can rise, or someone might feel anxious. If you sense the other person is uneasy, you can address their concerns directly by asking if they want clarification or a short break.

On your side, emotional intelligence helps you control your impulses. If the other side says something you dislike, you do not have to snap back. You can pause, take a breath, and respond in a calm manner. When you maintain emotional stability, you show professionalism and keep the talk focused on solving the problem at hand.

5.6 The Role of Empathy in Communication

Empathy is trying to see things from the other side's perspective. If they sense that you care about their needs, they are more likely to listen to your requests. Sometimes, people think empathy is a sign of weakness. In reality, empathy can be a strength because it helps you craft arguments that resonate better with the other side.

Practical ways to show empathy:

1. **Acknowledgment**: Say something like, "I understand you need to keep costs under control."
2. **Validation**: "I see why that deadline is important to your project."
3. **Openness**: Invite them to share more details about their worries or goals.

Empathy does not mean you agree to everything they want. It means you recognize why they want it. This understanding can help you propose solutions that feel more balanced and logical to them.

5.7 Building Rapport Through Communication

Rapport is a sense of connection or harmony between people. It can make a negotiation smoother because both sides feel comfortable talking honestly. A big part of building rapport is treating the other side with respect.

- **Use Their Name**: People generally respond well when you say their name in conversation, as long as you do not overdo it.
- **Show Genuine Interest**: If they mention a concern about timing or budget, ask a follow-up question.
- **Positive Body Language**: While Chapter 7 will address body language in detail, a simple nod or a small friendly smile can reinforce your verbal communication.

Rapport is often about small signals of respect. Even if you disagree on many points, showing basic politeness helps keep the door open for productive talks.

5.8 Overcoming Communication Barriers

Sometimes, barriers arise that disrupt communication. These barriers can be physical (like a noisy environment) or related to differences in language or background. They can also be personal barriers, like bias or lack of trust.

1. **Physical Barriers**: If the room is noisy or if the internet connection is weak, fix those issues first. Clear communication requires a setting where you can hear and be heard.
2. **Language Barriers**: If there is a language difference, consider having a translator or using simpler words.
3. **Bias**: Try to put aside assumptions you might have about the person you are negotiating with. Treat them as an individual, not a stereotype.
4. **Trust Issues**: If trust is low, the other side might doubt your statements. Be transparent where you can, and avoid exaggerations that could worsen mistrust.

When you spot a communication barrier, address it promptly. The longer it lingers, the more it can weaken the negotiation process.

5.9 Summaries and Paraphrasing to Confirm Understanding

One of the best ways to avoid misunderstandings is to summarize or paraphrase what you have heard. For instance, if the other side says, "We need the shipment by the first of next month, and we need the cost to be under $5,000," you can respond with something like, "So, you are looking for a delivery date of around the first of next month, with a total cost of $5,000 or less. Is that right?" This gives them a chance to confirm or correct your interpretation.

Benefits of paraphrasing:

- It shows you are paying attention.
- It uncovers any points where your understanding might be off.
- It reduces the chance of disputes later about what was said.

Paraphrasing also makes the other side feel heard, which can build trust and make them more open to your requests.

5.10 The Role of Questions in Communication

Good questions drive a negotiation forward. While we will cover listening in more detail in the next chapter, it is also important to see how questions form part of communication fundamentals. There are two main types of questions:

1. **Open-Ended Questions**: These invite longer responses. Example: "How can we make the timeline more flexible for both sides?"
2. **Closed-Ended Questions**: These can be answered with a yes or no. Example: "Would you agree to a small extension if we provide a discount?"

Use open-ended questions when you want the other side to explain or explore options. Use closed-ended questions when you need clarity or to confirm specifics. By balancing the two, you can lead the conversation in a structured way.

5.11 Handling Interruptions and Distractions

Negotiations can sometimes be interrupted. A phone might ring, or someone might need to step out. These disruptions break the flow of communication, leading to confusion or lost momentum.

Ways to handle interruptions:

1. **Pause**: If you are in the middle of a key point, stop speaking until you can regain everyone's attention.
2. **Recap**: Once the interruption is over, briefly restate your last point to ensure nothing is missed.
3. **Reschedule**: If interruptions are constant, it might be better to find another time or place where everyone can focus fully.

Distractions can also be mental, such as the other side checking their phone or email. If you notice they are not paying attention, politely ask if you should continue or if they need a moment. This direct approach can remind them of the importance of staying engaged.

5.12 Digital vs. Face-to-Face Communication

Many negotiations now happen online or by phone. While technology can save time, it can also create new communication challenges. Emails, for instance, lack tone of voice and facial cues, which can lead to misunderstandings. Video calls offer some visual clues, but technical problems can still disrupt the flow.

1. **Email**: Great for summarizing agreements in writing, but can lead to confusion if the language is not precise.
2. **Phone Calls**: Allow real-time conversation, but you cannot see body language or facial expressions.
3. **Video Calls**: Combine audio and visual, but connection issues or camera angles can limit nonverbal clarity.

In each case, the key is clarity. Write or speak in a straightforward manner and do not assume the other side understands your tone. If a conversation becomes tense via email, consider switching to a call or meeting in person to clear things up.

5.13 Strategies for Guiding the Conversation

A skilled negotiator often guides the conversation rather than letting it wander. One way to do this is by setting an agenda at the start and politely steering the talk back to it whenever it goes off track. For instance, if the other side begins discussing an unrelated topic, you can say, "That is an interesting point, but can we return to the timeline issue first?"

Another strategy is to use transitions. For example: "We have covered the cost details. Now, let us move on to the delivery schedule." These transitions keep the discussion organized and show that you have a structure in mind. The other side is less likely to get lost if you give clear signals about the direction of the conversation.

5.14 The Difference Between Persuasion and Manipulation

Persuasion involves using logical arguments and fair tactics to influence the other person's viewpoint. Manipulation involves tricking or misleading them. In negotiations, manipulation can harm trust. If the other side realizes you have used unfair tactics, they might walk away or demand much stricter terms.

Persuasion focuses on aligning your interests with the other side's interests, showing how both can benefit. It relies on facts, clear communication, and empathy. For example, you might say, "If we move the deadline a week sooner, you will have more time to roll out your new product before the holiday rush." That is a persuasive statement that points out a real advantage.

5.15 Maintaining Calm Under Pressure

Pressure can come from aggressive tactics, a tight deadline, or a high-stakes situation. When people feel pressured, they might talk faster, lose track of their main points, or say things they regret. Communication fundamentals include staying calm and collected, even when tensions rise.

- **Take a Breath**: A small pause can prevent an outburst.
- **Speak Slowly**: This keeps you in control of your message.
- **Stay Polite**: Even if the other side is rude, do not reply in the same way. That can escalate the situation.

When you remain composed, your words carry more weight. The other side sees that you are not easily rattled, which can encourage a more balanced discussion.

5.16 Adapting to Different Communication Styles

People vary in how they talk and listen. Some like direct statements; others prefer a more diplomatic approach. Some people are very expressive, using a lot of gestures, while others speak with a steady demeanor. Adjusting to someone's communication style can make them feel more at ease.

- **Direct Communicators**: They want concise statements. If you go off-topic, they might become impatient.
- **Indirect Communicators**: They may speak around an issue rather than stating it plainly. Listen carefully for clues to what they truly want.
- **Detail-Oriented Communicators**: They might need data, charts, and thorough explanations.
- **Big-Picture Communicators**: They might prefer broad ideas and future possibilities rather than small details.

Watch how the other side responds. If they seem frustrated by your style, consider adjusting. This does not mean changing your personality; it means packaging your message in a way they can digest easily.

5.17 Cultural Sensitivities in Communication

Culture can shape how people express themselves. Some cultures value direct statements, while others see directness as too blunt. Some cultures expect a period of polite talk before discussing business; others prefer getting straight to the point. If you are negotiating with someone from another cultural background, it is wise to do some research in advance.

1. **Greetings and Formalities**: In some places, titles and formal greetings matter a lot.
2. **Pauses and Silence**: In certain cultures, silence is a sign of careful thought. In others, it may be uncomfortable.
3. **Personal Distance**: Standing too close or too far can affect how comfortable someone feels.

Learning these small details can help you avoid accidental offenses. It also shows respect, which can lead to smoother talks.

5.18 Combining Clarity with Flexibility

While clarity is essential, you also need to be flexible. If you lock in on one communication style, you might miss the chance to connect with the other side in a better way. For example, you might prepare a very logical presentation, but then realize they respond more to personal stories or examples. Adapting on the fly can yield better results.

Flexibility also means adjusting your tone if you sense the other person is feeling pressured or confused. You can slow down, invite them to ask questions, or shift the topic temporarily to break tension. By being flexible, you show that you are not just pushing your own agenda but also considering how to keep the conversation balanced.

5.19 Finalizing Agreements with Clear Language

When you are close to an agreement, do not let confusion sabotage your progress. Summarize the key terms clearly:

- **State each point**: For example, price, delivery date, and any special conditions.
- **Ask for confirmation**: "Do we both agree on these points?"
- **Write it down**: If it is a complex agreement, confirm it in writing, even if just in an email recap.

A good final statement might be: "We have settled on a total cost of $3,000, delivery by April 1st, and a 90-day warranty. Is that correct?" This approach leaves little room for misunderstanding. If both sides confirm, you have a solid verbal agreement that can be turned into an official contract or document.

5.20 Golden Gem and Closing Thoughts

Golden gem: When you notice the conversation going off track or becoming too heated, guide it back with a simple phrase like, "Let's refocus on the main issue." This small step can save a lot of time and help both sides remain calm.

Communication fundamentals set the tone for everything that happens in a negotiation. If you master clarity, respect, and empathy, you will create an environment where issues are solved more smoothly. Whether you are dealing with a small personal matter or a major business deal, strong communication skills will serve you well.

In the next chapter, we will look at the other side of the communication coin: listening. Good speakers also know how to pay attention when someone else is talking. By learning how to listen effectively, you can catch hidden clues about what the other side truly wants, which leads to smarter and more efficient deals.

Chapter 6: Listening Skills

Communication is a two-way path. While talking is one part of the equation, listening is the other. In fact, many negotiators say that listening is even more crucial than speaking. If you fail to pick up on key details or signals, you might miss the real reasons behind the other side's requests. This chapter will teach you how to listen in a way that promotes trust, uncovers hidden needs, and encourages a smoother path to agreement.

We will explore the difference between hearing and active listening, how to show you are paying attention, and methods to confirm that you understand what has been said. We will also cover practical tips, like handling awkward silences and managing your own urge to jump in with quick responses. By the end, you will see how strong listening skills can give you insights that lead to better negotiation outcomes.

6.1 Hearing vs. Active Listening

"Hearing" means your ears detect sound, but "active listening" means you are fully focused on the words, tone, and intent. It includes observing the speaker's body language and noticing small shifts in their emotions. When you practice active listening, you do not just sit silently; you use small verbal or nonverbal cues to show you are engaged.

Traits of active listening:

1. **Concentration**: You are not checking your phone or letting your mind wander.
2. **Acknowledgment**: You say short affirmations like "Yes" or nod your head to show you are following.
3. **Reflection**: You try to understand the emotion behind the words, not just the facts.

Active listening helps you spot underlying concerns or motives. For example, if the other side repeatedly brings up deadlines, it might mean their biggest worry is timing. That clue could become your leverage point: if you can meet their schedule, they might be more flexible on price.

6.2 Benefits of Effective Listening in Negotiation

1. **Builds Trust**: When people feel you are paying close attention, they are more likely to share honest details.
2. **Reduces Errors**: You avoid misunderstandings that could lead to costly mistakes.
3. **Uncovers Hidden Interests**: Often, the other side has deeper concerns than what they first mention. Good listening reveals these concerns, giving you a chance to address them.
4. **Encourages Reciprocity**: If you listen well, the other side may feel obligated to listen to you more carefully in return.

Listening is not just a polite gesture; it is a strategic tool. By letting them speak and clarifying their points, you gather information that helps shape your next move.

6.3 Barriers to Good Listening

Even if you want to listen, several barriers can get in the way:

1. **Preoccupation**: You might be thinking about your next statement rather than focusing on what they are saying.
2. **Personal Bias**: If you have strong opinions, you might dismiss or distort the other side's words.
3. **Emotional Reactions**: Feeling angry or anxious can stop you from absorbing information.
4. **External Distractions**: Noise, phone alerts, or side conversations.

To overcome these barriers, you can practice self-awareness. For instance, if you notice yourself thinking about your response while they are talking, consciously bring your focus back to their words. If outside noise is a problem, suggest moving to a quieter area.

6.4 Techniques for Better Listening

1. The 3-Second Pause
After the other side finishes a statement, wait a few seconds before you respond. This small pause ensures you do not cut them off if they are just pausing to breathe, and it gives you a moment to reflect.

2. Ask Clarifying Questions
Simple questions like, "Could you tell me more about that?" or "When you say 'urgent,' how soon do you mean?" can help ensure you grasp the details.

3. Use Minimal Encouragers
Phrases like "Yes," "I see," or "That makes sense" let them know you are following along. These are small signals that you are with them, not daydreaming.

4. Summarize
When they finish explaining, restate in your own words to check if you understood correctly. "So you are saying that the main issue is the lack of clear payment terms, right?" They will confirm or correct you, and that helps avoid errors.

6.5 Nonverbal Signals of Listening

While we will have a separate chapter on body language, a few key nonverbal signals show that you are paying attention:

- **Eye Contact**: Gently keep your gaze on the speaker's face, without staring aggressively.
- **Nods**: A small nod every now and then encourages them to continue.
- **Leaning Forward**: This posture can indicate interest.
- **Limiting Fidgeting**: Constantly checking your watch or phone suggests boredom.

These signals work together with your verbal cues to assure the speaker that you value what they have to say. Even if you disagree, showing genuine attention helps keep the discussion respectful.

6.6 Listening to Spot Opportunities

Many people talk about their problems or concerns in a negotiation without directly stating what they really want. A skilled listener picks up on clues to find opportunities. For example, they might say, "We have been disappointed by late deliveries in the past." If you catch that, you can offer a guarantee of on-time shipment to ease their worry. That guarantee might become your advantage, letting you secure better terms on other aspects.

To do this, pay special attention to repeated words or themes. If they mention "risk" multiple times, that might be their prime concern. Showing you can reduce risk could lead them to accept your price or other requests more easily.

6.7 Handling Emotional Outbursts

Sometimes, the other side might become upset or frustrated. They could raise their voice or make harsh statements. In these moments, how you listen can calm the situation. Instead of matching their anger, keep your voice steady and acknowledge their feelings. You might say, "I understand this is a serious issue for you. Let's talk about what we can do to address it."

By doing this, you focus on the problem instead of their emotional display. You do not have to agree with everything they say, but by showing you hear their concern, you might help them calm down and move back to a more logical discussion.

6.8 Cultural Nuances in Listening

In some cultures, interrupting to clarify is seen as normal. In others, interrupting might be very rude. Some people pause often while they speak, which might be mistaken for them finishing their turn. Learning about the cultural norms of the other side can help you avoid cutting them off or seeming impatient. If you are unsure, it is usually safer to wait longer than you think before jumping in.

If there is a language difference, be extra mindful. They might need more time to find the right words. If something sounds unclear, politely ask for clarification rather than guessing. This patience can prevent misunderstandings and show respect for their effort to communicate in a language that may not be their first.

6.9 Listening to What Is Not Said

Sometimes, the most important points are those the other side avoids mentioning. For example, if you keep asking about a deadline and they change the subject, it might mean the deadline is flexible, or it might mean they are hiding details about it. If you notice repeated avoidance, that is a clue you can explore further.

Another sign is inconsistent information. If they mention a budget limit in one part of the conversation but later suggest a higher amount, there might be an unspoken reason. Listening carefully for these inconsistencies can help you spot negotiation levers. Be tactful when questioning these points, so they do not feel accused.

6.10 Balancing Listening with Speaking

While listening is crucial, you still need to speak up about your own needs. If you only listen and never share your perspective, the other side might assume you do not have strong positions. The best negotiators find a balance. They gather information by listening, then use that information to frame their requests in a way that addresses what they learned.

For instance, if the other side's main worry is cutting costs, you might tailor your offer to show how your solution saves money in the long run. But to do that effectively, you first have to listen enough to understand that cost reduction is their priority.

6.11 Signs You Are Not Listening Well

It helps to spot warning signs in your own behavior that suggest you are not truly listening. These might include:

- **Repeating Yourself**: If you keep restating points instead of responding to what they said.
- **Interrupting Often**: Cutting them off can signal you value your words more than theirs.
- **Changing the Subject**: If you steer the conversation away from their point without addressing it, they might feel ignored.
- **Confusion**: If you frequently ask them to repeat themselves, it could mean your mind is elsewhere.

Try to catch these habits and correct them mid-conversation. A quick mental note to yourself—"Focus!"—can bring you back to attentive listening.

6.12 The Power of Silence

Many people feel uncomfortable with silence. They rush to fill the gap with words. But in negotiation, a short silence can work in your favor. After you pose a question, waiting quietly can give the other side space to think. They might reveal more details than they planned because they want to break the silence.

Silence also shows you are not desperate to speak. If you calmly wait, it signals that you are considering their words carefully. This can make them more respectful of your eventual response. Just be sure not to let a pause become so long that it turns awkward. A few seconds can be enough to let them gather their thoughts.

6.13 Reflective Listening for Clarity

Reflective listening is a method where you repeat or paraphrase the core of what you heard, but in a way that encourages the other side to confirm or expand. For instance, if they say, "We are concerned about the stability of the product," you might respond: "You want to ensure that the product will last a long time without breaking down, correct?"

This technique not only confirms understanding but also encourages the speaker to keep going. They might add details you missed. Reflective listening feels supportive because it tells them you find their viewpoint important enough to restate carefully.

6.14 Listening in Group Negotiations

When multiple people are involved, listening becomes even more challenging. Voices can overlap, or certain individuals might dominate the conversation. One method is to ask each person to speak in turn. You can say, "Let's hear from each of you about your main concern, then we'll discuss them one by one."

As a listener in a group setting:

- Focus on the speaker at that moment.
- Take brief notes if needed, so you do not mix up people's statements.
- Summarize the group's points at key intervals, so everyone remains on the same page.

In group talks, confusion can spread fast if listening is neglected. Clear listening and summarizing can keep the discussion organized.

6.15 Strategies for Listening Under Stress

High-stress negotiations can make it hard to listen. Your mind might race with fears about the outcome or with anger at the other side's demands. To remain a good listener under stress:

1. **Breathe**: Take slow, deep breaths to calm yourself.

2. **Park Your Feelings**: Imagine setting your personal feelings aside for the moment so you can fully absorb their words.
3. **Repeat Important Details**: If they mention a vital point, quietly repeat it to yourself in your head.
4. **Look for Solutions**: Even if you disagree, approach their statements with the thought, "How could this lead to a solution?"

Listening under stress is a practice that gets better with time. You might start by using these steps in lower-stakes talks until they become second nature.

6.16 Avoiding Mind Reading

People often assume they know the other side's motives or feelings without actually hearing them out. This is called mind reading, and it can derail a negotiation. For example, you might think, "They only want to waste my time," or "They are not really serious about this deal." Those assumptions can make you dismiss their words prematurely.

A better approach is to let them explain their position fully. If you suspect something, you can ask a direct question: "Could you clarify what your main purpose is in seeking this type of solution?" You might be surprised to learn your assumption was off-base.

6.17 Listening for Nonverbal Cues

Even though Chapter 7 will delve deeper into body language, a listener should also keep an eye on the speaker's nonverbal signals:

- **Facial Expressions**: A slight frown or raised eyebrow might signal confusion or doubt.
- **Hand Gestures**: If they are gesturing a lot, they might be passionate or stressed.
- **Posture Changes**: Leaning back can signal disagreement or disinterest.

By noting these cues, you can ask a clarifying question: "You seem concerned. Can you tell me what is on your mind?" This approach invites them to share, rather than leaving you guessing.

6.18 Giving the Other Side Space to Talk

Some negotiators make the mistake of dominating the conversation. They assume that if they keep talking, they can control the outcome. But this can backfire because they learn less about the other side's concerns. By giving the other side space to talk, you gather the information you need to shape better deals.

Methods to let them speak more:

1. **Ask Open Questions**: "What else would help you decide?"
2. **Encourage Details**: "Can you walk me through how this issue affects your daily operations?"
3. **Resist Filling Pauses**: If they pause, wait a moment to see if they want to add more.

Often, the other side will reveal key details when they feel safe to speak at length.

6.19 Applying Listening Skills to Different Contexts

Negotiations happen in many areas of life, and listening skills help in each context:

- **Business Deals**: Understand client requirements clearly.
- **Salary Discussions**: Hear your boss's perspective on budget constraints.
- **Family Decisions**: Let everyone share their feelings about a joint purchase or holiday plan.
- **Community Projects**: Listen to neighbors' ideas and concerns before finalizing a plan.

In each of these, the principle remains the same: the better you listen, the more relevant information you gather, and the better your final decisions can be.

6.20 Golden Gem and Conclusion

Golden gem: When someone finishes speaking, try to wait a beat or two before responding. This short silence often encourages them to add extra details or clarifications that could be vital to reaching a good deal.

Listening is not just about being polite. It is a powerful negotiation tool that can reveal hidden interests, ease tension, and open pathways to solutions. By mastering active listening, you can stay one step ahead because you will know not just what the other side says, but why they say it.

In the next chapter, we will turn our focus to reading and using body language. While listening captures verbal content, body language can reveal insights that words alone do not provide. When you combine strong listening skills with an understanding of nonverbal signals, you gain a more complete view of what is really happening in the conversation.

Chapter 7: Body Language in Negotiations

Body language is a major part of communication that goes beyond words. During a negotiation, you send signals through your posture, hand gestures, facial expressions, and eye contact. The other side also sends signals, whether they realize it or not. Learning to read and control these signals can give you a significant advantage. You can spot when someone is uncomfortable, enthusiastic, or uncertain—sometimes before they even say a word.

In this chapter, we will explore how body language works in negotiations. We will discuss the importance of posture, the power of eye contact, the effects of gestures, and how to handle physical distance. We will also look at some common signs that may indicate stress, dishonesty, or confidence. By the end of this chapter, you will have a practical understanding of how to observe nonverbal signals and how to adjust your own signals for a more successful interaction.

7.1 The Importance of Nonverbal Communication

Nonverbal signals often speak louder than words. Studies show that a large percentage of human communication is transmitted through body language, tone of voice, and facial expressions. When you focus only on what people say, you might miss key clues.

In negotiations, these clues can tell you if someone agrees with you but is hesitant to say it, or if someone is uncertain about their own statements. For example, a person might say they are confident about a contract but show micro-expressions of doubt. If you spot that, you can adapt your approach, possibly offering reassurances or asking follow-up questions that get them to open up.

7.2 Reading Posture

Your overall posture sets a tone for how others see you and how you feel about yourself. Standing or sitting upright, with your shoulders back, often conveys confidence. Slouching or hunching may suggest low energy or insecurity.

Common Posture Signals

1. **Open Posture**: Arms uncrossed, torso facing the other side, shoulders relaxed. This generally shows you are ready to talk.
2. **Closed Posture**: Arms folded tightly or turning your body away. This can indicate defensive feelings, discomfort, or disagreement.
3. **Leaning Forward**: Suggests keen interest in what is being said.
4. **Leaning Back**: Can mean you are relaxed, or it can show disagreement or skepticism if done with folded arms.

Consider posture a tool. If you notice the other side suddenly shifts from an open posture to a closed one, it might mean something you said bothered them. You can gently ask if they have any concerns or if something is unclear. That allows you to address issues before they escalate.

7.3 Eye Contact

Eye contact is one of the clearest signals of attention and confidence. Maintaining appropriate eye contact shows you are engaged and trustworthy. Avoiding eye contact can appear suspicious or uneasy, though in some cultures frequent eye contact can feel too intense. The trick is to hold eye contact just long enough to show interest, but not so long that it becomes uncomfortable.

- **Steady Gaze**: Looking into someone's eyes with a calm expression can build a sense of connection.
- **Frequent Glances Away**: Might indicate nervousness or boredom. However, remember that some people naturally look away when thinking.

- **Blink Rate**: Rapid blinking can suggest stress or that the other person feels pressured.

If you notice someone looks down after making a statement, you can ask a polite question: "Would you like to clarify that point?" or "Is there any detail you want to add?" This gentle prompt might encourage them to share more, which can lead to deeper insights.

7.4 Facial Expressions

Facial expressions can change quickly, revealing emotions that words may hide. Some people have very expressive faces; others keep a neutral look. Here are a few common signals:

1. **Smiling**: A genuine smile can indicate warmth or agreement. A forced smile might be used to mask stress.
2. **Frowning**: Shows displeasure or confusion.
3. **Raised Eyebrows**: Often a sign of surprise or a request for more information.
4. **Tight Lips**: Can suggest tension, anger, or withholding of information.

Pay attention to micro-expressions—fleeting facial changes that happen in a split second. If you see a brief flicker of annoyance cross someone's face, it could mean your last statement hit a nerve. You can respond by calmly asking if they have concerns about what was just said.

7.5 Hand Gestures

Hands can either reinforce your points or send unplanned messages about your mood. Wild, fast movements can show excitement or agitation. Smooth, controlled gestures can give an impression of steadiness.

- **Open Palms**: Suggest honesty and openness.
- **Pointing Fingers**: Can appear accusing or aggressive, so use caution.

- **Steepling Fingers**: Touching the fingertips of both hands together in a peak can show confidence or a sense of authority.
- **Clenched Fists**: Can signal anger or frustration.

When you talk, try to use gestures that match your words. If you are stating a fact, keep your gestures calm and direct. If you are showing enthusiasm about an idea, a slightly more animated gesture can make you appear sincere. But avoid excessive hand movements that distract from your words.

7.6 Mirroring and Matching

Mirroring is when you subtly copy the other person's body language. This can happen naturally when two people feel comfortable with each other. For example, if they lean forward slightly, you might lean forward too. Doing this in a gentle way can build rapport because it signals empathy.

However, avoid making it obvious. If you mirror every movement like a mimic, it will appear strange. The goal is to create a sense of harmony, not to copy them exactly. Sometimes, if you notice the other person is tense, you can try shifting to a more relaxed position. Often, they will subconsciously follow you, and the conversation might become less strained.

7.7 Personal Space and Distance

Personal space is the comfortable distance between you and the other side. Going too close can be seen as aggressive or intrusive, while standing too far might suggest you are not engaged. This can differ across cultures and personal preferences.

- **Intimate Distance**: Usually reserved for close family or friends.
- **Personal Distance**: Used for conversations between friends or colleagues.
- **Social Distance**: Common in business settings.

- **Public Distance**: For speaking to a group or crowd.

In a negotiation setting, a social distance is often best—about a few feet apart if you are standing, or across a normal-sized table if you are seated. Watch for signs that the other person is uncomfortable. If they lean back or move their chair away, you might be too close.

7.8 Spotting Signs of Stress or Dishonesty

While there is no universal "tell" that someone is lying, certain signals can hint at discomfort or evasiveness:

1. **Touching the Face or Neck**: Some people touch or scratch their nose or neck when unsure or stressed.
2. **Fidgeting**: Tapping fingers, shifting feet, or playing with objects can reveal tension.
3. **Vocal Changes**: A higher pitch or cracking voice might appear under stress.
4. **Mixed Signals**: Their words say one thing, but their body language suggests another (e.g., they say "Yes," but shake their head).

If you see these signs, do not jump to accusations. Instead, ask clarifying questions or gently explore the topic they seem uncomfortable discussing. This might lead them to reveal more or explain why they feel stressed.

7.9 Using Body Language to Show Confidence

Confidence can encourage the other side to take your statements more seriously. To appear confident:

- **Stand or Sit Up Straight**: Keep your spine aligned and your shoulders relaxed.
- **Keep Your Head Up**: Avoid dropping your chin toward your chest.
- **Use Smooth Movements**: Move purposefully rather than in a jerky manner.

- **Avoid Overly Defensive Positions**: Try not to cross your arms for long periods unless you are cold or it is your natural resting posture.

A calm, confident demeanor can subtly influence the other side to assume you have solid reasons behind your requests. In turn, they might approach discussions more respectfully.

7.10 Calming Body Language When Tension Rises

Negotiations can become heated or stressful. Using soothing body language can help cool down the atmosphere:

- **Gentle Hand Gestures**: Palms up or slightly open can show a willingness to find a middle ground.
- **Small Nod**: Indicates you acknowledge their points, even if you do not fully agree.
- **Slower Breathing**: If you breathe deeply and slowly, your body relaxes, and you project a calmer presence.
- **Limited Sudden Movements**: Quick or sharp gestures can escalate tension.

If you feel your own stress building, pause and take a slow breath before you speak. This short moment can help you maintain a composed expression and voice.

7.11 Dealing with Aggressive Body Language

Some negotiators might stare intensely, lean in aggressively, or use domineering gestures. They may be trying to intimidate or assert dominance. Responding calmly is key. If you mirror aggression with aggression, the situation can spiral.

- **Stay Steady**: Keep your posture upright but relaxed.
- **Maintain Polite Eye Contact**: Do not overly stare back, but do not look away timidly.

- **Use an Even Tone**: Keep your voice level to show you are not rattled.
- **Suggest a Pause**: If the atmosphere is too charged, request a short break. This can break the cycle of aggression.

By controlling your own body language, you show that intimidation does not sway you. This can encourage the other side to switch to a more balanced approach.

7.12 Interpreting Group Body Language

In a group negotiation, watch how team members on the other side interact with each other. Do they exchange glances when a certain topic is mentioned? Does one person shift uncomfortably whenever another speaks?

- **Leader Cues**: Often, there is a main decision-maker. Watch how others look at that person. They may look for approval before agreeing to something.
- **Disagreements**: If two people on the same team avoid eye contact or turn their bodies away from each other, there may be an internal conflict.
- **Group Synchronization**: If they move or react in unison, it may mean they have a well-rehearsed strategy.

By noticing these subtle dynamics, you can tailor your arguments or questions more precisely. For instance, if one member seems to hold the real power, direct more key points toward them.

7.13 Virtual Negotiations and Body Language

Nowadays, many negotiations happen via video calls. While you cannot see a person's entire body, you can still pick up cues:

- **Facial Expressions**: The face is usually visible, so watch for micro-expressions.

- **Eye Contact with the Camera**: Looking at the camera simulates direct eye contact. Looking away too much might seem distracted.
- **Posture on Camera**: Even if you are sitting at a desk, try to sit upright.
- **Hand Gestures**: Make sure your gestures are within the camera frame if you use them.

Technical issues can interrupt or hide body language signals. If the call is lagging or the video is grainy, clarify any points in doubt. You might say, "I noticed you looked a bit concerned. Did you have a question about what I just said?" to confirm what you saw was accurate.

7.14 Cultural Differences in Body Language

Culture can influence how people use and interpret body language. For example, in some cultures, direct eye contact is a sign of respect, while in others it can be seen as confrontational. Personal space can also vary across cultures—what is acceptable in one place might be too close in another.

Before negotiating with someone from a different cultural background, do some research on basic nonverbal norms. During the meeting, stay attentive for signs that they might be uncomfortable with your mannerisms. If you sense confusion, adjust your behavior slightly to respect their norms.

7.15 Practice and Self-Awareness

Improving your own body language starts with self-awareness. Many people do not realize they fidget, slouch, or display distracting gestures. You might consider practicing in front of a mirror or recording yourself:

- **Record a Mock Session**: Watch the video to see how you hold yourself and if you make any odd gestures.

- **Seek Feedback**: Ask a friend or colleague to observe you during a practice negotiation. They can point out habits you might not notice.
- **Make Small Adjustments**: Focus on one or two improvements at a time, such as keeping your back straight or using calmer hand movements.

Over time, you will build a more confident and controlled presence. This can help you feel more comfortable, which often leads to better negotiation performance.

7.16 Managing Nervous Energy

Negotiations can be stressful, especially if high stakes are involved. Nervous energy often shows up as shaking hands, bouncing legs, or pacing.

Ways to channel nervous energy:

1. **Grounding Techniques**: Place both feet on the floor, sit up, and breathe slowly to feel more secure.
2. **Relaxation Exercises**: Take a few deep breaths, inhaling through the nose and exhaling through the mouth.
3. **Use a Pen or a Pad**: Gently hold a pen or jot down notes to occupy your hands so they do not fidget as much.
4. **Positive Self-Talk**: Remind yourself that you have prepared and have valuable points to share.

Small signs of nervousness are normal and can even be seen as sincerity. Just try to keep them from overwhelming your body language.

7.17 Adapting Your Body Language to the Negotiation Phase

Negotiations often follow a sequence: opening statements, information exchange, bargaining, and closure. Your body language can shift slightly at each stage:

1. **Opening**: Show friendliness and openness to set a positive tone. Smile, maintain good eye contact, and have open posture.
2. **Information Exchange**: Lean forward a bit to show active listening. Nod to encourage the speaker.
3. **Bargaining**: Display calm confidence. Use gestures to highlight key points. Control your facial expressions to avoid showing panic or impatience.
4. **Closure**: When agreement is near, keep your posture assured but remain open to any last-minute questions or clarifications.

This phased approach signals that you are engaged and flexible without appearing unstable in your demeanor.

7.18 Responding to Mixed Signals

Sometimes, the other person's words and body language conflict. They might say they are happy to move forward, but they look tense or avoid eye contact. This is a sign you should check for unresolved issues.

You can address the mix by asking a neutral question: "It seems there might be a concern we have not covered. Is there something you would like to discuss?" This approach avoids accusing them of lying. Instead, it opens the door for them to share any reservations.

7.19 Ethical Use of Body Language

Using body language in negotiations should be about clarity and better understanding, not manipulation. If you pretend confidence you do not have or try to mimic sincerity you do not feel, you risk being discovered. Once the other side suspects fake behavior, trust can be hard to rebuild.

Focus on genuine listening and presenting yourself honestly but in the best possible light. Avoid tactics like false flattery or intentionally misleading gestures. Ethical communication builds credibility, which can pay off in long-term relationships.

7.20 Conclusion and Golden Gem

Body language is a powerful layer of communication that can either reinforce or contradict your words. By understanding posture, eye contact, gestures, and expressions, you can gain insights into how the other side feels. You can also manage your own signals to project confidence, calm, and openness.

Golden gem: If you notice someone's nonverbal cues shift suddenly—like their eyes dart away or their posture closes—pause and politely check if there is a concern they want to address. This small act shows attentiveness and may uncover critical information that could shape the final deal.

Up next, we will look at how to build trust and credibility (Chapter 8). Body language plays a role in trust, but there are many other actions you can take to reassure the other side of your honesty and expertise. By combining strong body language awareness with ethical behavior, you create an environment where both sides can negotiate more freely.

Chapter 8: Building Trust and Credibility

Trust and credibility are cornerstones of successful negotiations. Even if you have the best offer on the table, the other side may hesitate if they do not believe in your honesty or reliability. On the other hand, a strong sense of trust can encourage the other side to share more information, make fair concessions, or agree to terms they might otherwise doubt.

This chapter will explore the concept of trust in negotiations. We will examine how to earn credibility through honesty, consistency, and expertise. We will also look at how to repair trust if it gets damaged, and how small actions—like being on time or keeping promises—can set the stage for deeper cooperation. By the end, you should have a clear understanding of practical methods to establish yourself as a trustworthy negotiator.

8.1 Why Trust Matters

Trust sets the tone for how open or defensive each side becomes. When trust levels are high, parties feel safe exchanging information and exploring creative solutions. When trust is low, people hide details or fear that the other side will exploit any weakness.

In some negotiations, especially long-term partnerships, building trust can matter as much as the deal itself. A partner who trusts you will likely seek you out for future opportunities or recommend you to others. Conversely, if trust is broken, word can spread quickly, making it harder for you to negotiate effectively in the future.

8.2 Defining Credibility

Credibility is the belief that you have the knowledge and skills to back up your statements. It combines expertise (you know what you are talking about) and reliability (you say what you mean and follow through on promises). Credibility can come from your track record, your qualifications, or the way you present your case.

For instance, a financial consultant who consistently provides accurate forecasts gains credibility. Their clients trust that when they propose a deal, it is based on solid data. In a personal context, a neighbor who always keeps the yard tidy and returns borrowed tools on time builds credibility as a reliable person.

8.3 Honesty as a Foundation

Honesty is a direct path to trust. If you are caught in even a small lie—like inflating your background or fudging numbers—the other side may question everything else you say. While you do not have to reveal every strategic detail, blatant falsehoods can ruin your reputation.

- **Avoid Exaggerations**: Instead of claiming, "We are the best in the entire industry," cite specific awards or records.
- **Clarify Uncertainties**: If you do not know something, say so rather than guessing. Offer to provide more accurate information later.
- **Admit Mistakes**: If you made an error, acknowledge it. This can actually boost trust by showing accountability.

Honesty does not mean giving up your negotiation position. You can withhold certain details as long as you are not stating false information. Ethical negotiation allows for strategic silence, but not deception.

8.4 Consistency Between Words and Actions

A key element of trust is consistency: you do what you say you will do. If you promise to send documents by Friday, send them by Friday. If you claim you will follow up with new data, actually follow up.

Inconsistent behavior—such as making promises you do not keep or changing your statements without explanation—makes the other side uneasy. They start to wonder if your other claims are also unreliable. Consistency reassures them that you can be taken at your word.

8.5 Demonstrating Expertise

Showing expertise can raise your credibility. However, you must do so without sounding arrogant. Let your knowledge speak for itself through:

1. **Accurate Data and Facts**: Base your statements on solid research.
2. **Clear Explanations**: Break down complex ideas in straightforward language.
3. **Relevant Experience**: Briefly mention prior successful deals or projects that relate to the current negotiation.

For example, if you are discussing a web development project, you might say, "We have completed over 50 e-commerce websites with a 95% customer satisfaction rate." This statement is concise, factual, and proves you understand the field.

8.6 Demonstrating Fairness

Fairness is another trust-builder. If you appear to only chase your own gains at the other side's expense, they will be cautious. But if you make proposals that account for both parties' interests, they may see you as balanced.

- **Offer Win-Win Solutions**: If you find ways for both sides to benefit, it shows you value cooperation.
- **Listen to Their Concerns**: A fair negotiator does not dismiss the other side's difficulties.
- **Be Willing to Give**: If you request a concession, be ready to make one as well.

Fairness does not mean letting yourself be taken advantage of. It means showing you respect the interests of the other side as legitimate.

8.7 Transparency in Communication

While you may not reveal every detail of your strategy, being transparent about key points can build trust. For instance, if you have a strict deadline due to budget cycles, explain that. The other side might be more flexible if they understand why you need a faster decision.

Examples of transparency:

- Stating your main objective clearly: "We want to reduce our shipping costs by 10%."
- Acknowledging limitations: "Our budget cannot go above $50,000 for this phase."
- Sharing relevant data: "Here is the market report showing average pricing trends."

Transparency counters suspicion. It also reduces the risk of surprises, which can damage trust.

8.8 Body Language and Trust

As mentioned in Chapter 7, body language can convey honesty or deception. Consistent body language—calm posture, steady eye contact, genuine facial expressions—supports your spoken words. Shifty eyes or fidgeting might raise doubts, even if your words are truthful.

If you notice the other side acting uneasy, you can address it. "I sense there might be a concern about this part of the contract. Would you like to talk about it?" This open approach can ease tension and show that you value their comfort in the discussion.

8.9 Timing and Punctuality

Arriving late or delaying meetings without explanation chips away at trust. On the flip side, being punctual or, if needed, giving advance notice of a delay, shows respect for the other side's time. This simple habit can subtly reinforce your reliability.

If an unexpected problem arises, communicate right away. If you promise to give feedback on Thursday but realize you need more data, send a quick note explaining the delay and give a new date. This keeps expectations realistic and shows you are not ignoring your commitments.

8.10 Keeping Confidentiality

Trust can hinge on how well you protect sensitive information. If the other side shares proprietary data with you, do not disclose it without permission. Breaching confidentiality can end not just that deal but future opportunities as well.

- **Non-Disclosure Agreements (NDAs)**: If you sign one, make sure you honor it fully.
- **Limiting Access**: Only share the other side's data with team members who need to see it.
- **Clear Boundaries**: If you cannot keep certain information hidden (for legal reasons), let the other side know upfront.

Respecting privacy encourages the other side to open up more, which can lead to more productive negotiations.

8.11 Positive Relationship-Building

Trust is easier to establish if you show genuine interest in a good relationship. Some steps include:

- **Small Courtesies**: Using polite greetings, learning and using their name correctly.
- **Good Listening**: Let them speak without interruption, showing that their opinions matter.
- **Acknowledging Achievements**: If they mention a recent success, congratulate them briefly.

These might seem like small gestures, but they create a friendly atmosphere. Over time, these gestures accumulate into a sense of mutual respect, which supports trust.

8.12 Consistency Over Time

True credibility is not built overnight. It develops through repeated experiences where you prove yourself reliable. If this is the first time you are negotiating with someone, they might rely on your reputation from others who have worked with you. If you do not have an established reputation, you may have to work a bit harder to show consistency from the beginning.

In ongoing partnerships, keep your promises. If any changes occur, communicate them clearly and as soon as possible. Over multiple deals or interactions, the other side will see a pattern of trustworthy behavior.

8.13 Apologizing and Repairing Damage

Even the most careful negotiators can make mistakes or experience unforeseen problems. If you break a promise—maybe you could not deliver a report on time—admit it promptly. Apologize if necessary and offer a solution: "I'm sorry for the delay. I have arranged for an extended support period at no extra cost to make up for this inconvenience."

An honest apology plus a corrective action can sometimes increase trust because it shows accountability. However, repeated mistakes followed by apologies lose impact over time. Ultimately, consistent reliability is what sustains credibility.

8.14 Avoiding Manipulative Tactics

Some negotiators think they can be clever by using manipulation or deceit, like false deadlines or made-up competitors. While such moves might win a single deal, they harm trust in the long run. If the other side discovers they were deceived, they may refuse to do business again. They might also warn others about you.

Trustworthy negotiators focus on real facts and fair strategies. They may choose to keep certain information private, but they do not fabricate or lie. Maintaining ethical standards builds a solid reputation that can open doors to future opportunities.

8.15 The Role of Third-Party Validation

Sometimes, the other side wants proof that you are as good as you claim. If you have references, testimonials, or case studies, share them. A potential business partner might feel more reassured if they see that other clients were satisfied with your performance. In personal matters, mutual friends or a community leader's recommendation can serve the same purpose.

- **Testimonials**: Short quotes from past partners or clients praising your reliability.
- **Case Studies**: An overview of a previous project with results that highlight your expertise.
- **Professional Endorsements**: Membership in respected associations or certifications.

Using third-party validation is especially helpful when you are building trust with someone new who cannot gauge you from personal experience.

8.16 Being Respectful in Disagreements

Negotiations can involve conflicts of interest. It is possible to disagree while remaining respectful. When you respect the other side's views, they are less likely to see you as a threat, even if you do not share their opinion.

- **Separate People from Problems**: Focus on the issue, not on personal traits.
- **Use Polite Language**: "I see your point, but I have some concerns about the timeline."

- **Seek Common Ground**: "We both want to stay within budget, but we differ on how to do it."

This polite approach shows you are not dismissing them. Even if the outcome is not perfect, they can still respect you for handling disagreements maturely.

8.17 Transparency About Motives

Sometimes, stating your motives openly can reduce suspicion. For example, if you are pushing for a quick decision because your team needs to finalize next quarter's budget, say so. If you want to build a long-term partnership rather than a one-off sale, make that clear. This candor can help the other side understand your perspective and see that you are not hiding a hidden agenda.

If you realize your motive has changed—maybe you found a new partner or your budget constraints eased—update the other side. They may not like all changes, but they will trust you more if you keep them informed.

8.18 Handling Sensitive Topics with Care

In many negotiations, certain topics are delicate—like salaries, layoffs, or past conflicts. How you address these topics can build or break trust. Use a calm tone, present facts, and acknowledge emotions if needed. For example, if a client is upset about a past issue, say, "I understand that caused trouble for your team. Let us see how we can prevent that from happening again."

Do not dismiss or belittle their concerns. Offer a plan to address them, if possible. Even if the conversation is uncomfortable, handling it with honesty and respect can strengthen your credibility.

8.19 Monitoring and Checking In

Trust is not something you build once and forget. Keep an eye on the relationship. If you sense new tensions, check in: "Is everything going smoothly on your side? Let me know if there is any problem we can solve." This proactive approach shows you care about maintaining mutual confidence.

Periodic check-ins also allow you to spot small issues before they become large. For instance, if you have a shared project, a quick message like, "How is the progress on your end?" can reveal any hidden concerns that might affect trust if not addressed.

8.20 Conclusion and Golden Gem

Trust and credibility are not optional extras; they are central to a productive negotiation. When people trust you, they tend to share information more freely and consider your proposals with an open mind. By being consistent, fair, honest, and transparent, you create a strong base that leads to smoother talks and more stable agreements.

Golden gem: A sincere apology, combined with real action to fix the mistake, can not only restore trust but sometimes deepen it. Owning up to errors shows integrity, and integrity is a powerful element of credibility.

Next, we will move into handling emotions and conflict (Chapter 9). Trust plays a role in managing high-pressure moments. If both sides believe in each other's good faith, it is easier to work through tough disagreements without losing respect. By combining the trust-building steps in this chapter with conflict-resolution strategies, you will be better prepared for the most challenging aspects of negotiation.

Chapter 9: Handling Emotions and Conflict

Negotiations often involve strong feelings. When people care deeply about an outcome—perhaps money, pride, or control is at stake—tempers can flare. This chapter will show how to handle emotions and disagreements in a way that leads to more understanding, not less. Managing feelings well can help you stay calm, avoid destructive fights, and look for results that both sides can accept.

We will look at how to recognize signs of anger or stress in yourself and others, how to reduce tension during heated moments, and how to keep problems from getting worse. We will also cover techniques that help you separate the issue from the person. By the end of this chapter, you should have practical methods to tackle emotional roadblocks. This will help you keep discussions on track even when frustration levels climb.

9.1 Why Emotions Matter in Negotiation

Emotions affect how we process information. When someone is upset, they might ignore facts, twist words, or refuse to consider options they would normally find acceptable. On the other side, a person who feels calm and balanced might spot better solutions or remain open to compromise.

Emotions also affect trust. If a person thinks their feelings are not respected, they might pull away from talks or act out of spite rather than logic. By understanding how emotions work, you can reduce problems before they grow too big.

9.2 Recognizing Your Own Emotions

It is important to notice your own emotional state during a negotiation. Sometimes you might feel worried about losing a deal or angry if you think the other side is not listening. If you do not acknowledge these feelings, they can slip into your tone of voice or word choice. This can sabotage the discussion.

Tips to manage your own emotions:

1. **Pause and Breathe**: If you notice tension, take a slow breath. This tiny break can help you regain control.
2. **Stay Aware of Physical Signs**: Racing heartbeat, tense shoulders, or a flushed face can mean stress. Recognizing these signals early helps you step back.
3. **Use Self-Talk**: Remind yourself of your main goals. Tell yourself to focus on facts rather than blaming others.

9.3 Spotting Emotional Shifts in Others

Just as you have feelings, the other side does too. Watch for sudden changes in their body language or tone. Maybe their voice gets louder, they lean back with crossed arms, or they speak more rapidly than before. These might be signs of anger, frustration, or worry.

When you see these signs, do not ignore them. Pause the conversation and check in: "I sense this topic might be upsetting. Would you like to share your view in more detail?" This shows respect for their feelings and can keep tensions from escalating.

9.4 Common Causes of Conflict

In a negotiation, conflict usually comes from a few basic sources:

1. **Diverging Goals**: Each side wants something that appears incompatible.
2. **Miscommunication**: Misheard or misunderstood statements can spark arguments.
3. **Personality Clashes**: Different styles of speaking or decision-making can rub people the wrong way.

4. **Past History**: Unresolved issues from earlier deals or interactions might carry over.
5. **Perceived Unfairness**: If one side feels the other is taking advantage, frustration builds.

Understanding the root cause helps you address it directly rather than just dealing with the surface anger. If the conflict stems from a simple misunderstanding, clarifying the details can solve the main problem.

9.5 Separating the Person from the Problem

A key principle is to attack the problem, not the person. It is tempting to label the other side as "difficult" or "unreasonable." But doing so often increases conflict because they feel personally attacked.

Instead, focus on the issue at hand. For instance, if the conflict is about delivery times, keep the talk on scheduling facts rather than accusing them of being lazy or disorganized. This approach helps maintain respect. Even if they are at fault, frame it as a shared problem to solve rather than a personal flaw.

9.6 Techniques for Cooling Tension

When emotions start to boil, you can use a few strategies to ease things:

1. **Suggest a Short Break**: A 5-10 minute pause can help both sides calm down.
2. **Acknowledge Feelings**: Saying, "I see this is important to you," can reduce the other person's need to shout or push.
3. **Stay Quiet**: Sometimes letting them speak their mind without interruption is enough for them to feel heard and calm down.
4. **Ask Questions**: Seek more details about their concerns rather than just responding with counter-arguments.

These small actions can lower the temperature in the room, letting you return to a more cooperative tone.

9.7 Handling Personal Attacks

Unfortunately, some people resort to personal digs or insults when they feel cornered. If you are on the receiving end, it can be tough to stay calm. But answering with more insults only escalates the fight.

A better approach is to call out the attack without returning it. For example, calmly say, "I understand this is a difficult topic, but I prefer we keep the discussion focused on the issue rather than personal remarks." This politely but firmly shows you will not be drawn into name-calling.

If the insults persist, you might suggest a break or consider ending the session if the other side refuses to communicate respectfully.

9.8 Strategies for Negotiating Under Stress

Big deals or tight deadlines can heighten stress. Here is how to handle high-pressure talks:

- **Prepare Thoroughly**: Having clear facts and a plan reduces anxiety.
- **Delegate**: If you have a team, split tasks so no single person is overwhelmed.
- **Set Realistic Goals**: Pressure often comes from trying to achieve the impossible. Aim for goals that are high but still within reason.
- **Manage Time**: Rushing can create emotional tension. Build in short pauses if the conversation grows heated.

By having a structured approach, you reduce the risk of meltdown moments.

9.9 Dealing with Silent Anger

Sometimes, people show their anger through silence or passive resistance. They might say very little or keep nodding but never agree to anything in the final sense. This can be as damaging as open hostility because it prevents real progress.

To address silent anger:

1. **Invite Feedback**: "I want to hear your thoughts. Do you have any concerns about this point?"
2. **Gently Probe**: Ask if there is anything bothering them or if they feel uncomfortable about the deal.
3. **Offer a Private Talk**: If you are in a group setting, suggest speaking one-on-one. They might open up if they feel less exposed.

Recognizing silent anger helps you prevent unresolved tension from stalling the entire negotiation.

9.10 Understanding the Role of Ego

Ego often plays a role in conflicts. People do not like feeling they have "lost." Some negotiators fear that agreeing to certain terms makes them appear weak. This mindset can lead to stubborn stands, even if a deal might be good for both sides.

You can ease ego problems by framing the negotiation as a shared challenge. For instance, say, "We're both aiming to make this product launch a success," rather than, "I want to beat you on pricing." Using inclusive language can help keep egos in check.

9.11 Avoiding Emotional Traps

Certain tactics are designed to trigger emotional responses. Someone might use harsh deadlines ("Sign now or the deal is off"), guilt trips, or threats. These are emotional traps. They push you to respond in anger or panic.

Instead of reacting immediately:

1. **Acknowledge the Tactic**: "I see you're concerned about the timeline."
2. **Stay Firm on Facts**: Return to the actual data or terms.
3. **Stand Your Ground**: If they push too hard, calmly restate your position. If it feels abusive, consider walking away.

Not giving in to these traps helps you remain in control and keeps the discussion from spiraling.

9.12 Empathy vs. Sympathy

Empathy can cool down a tense moment. It means trying to see the situation from their perspective. For example, if they worry about budgets, say, "I understand it's tough when you have to manage so many costs." This shows respect for their viewpoint.

Sympathy, on the other hand, might go too far. You do not want to pity them; that can appear condescending. A balanced empathetic approach is best: "I understand why you're stressed, and I'd like to find a way to help both sides."

9.13 Converting Anger into Problem-Solving

Sometimes anger signals a real problem that has been ignored. If someone is angry about late payments, that frustration might hide deeper financial stress. By getting to the root of that anger, you can address the underlying issue.

Ask questions like, "What is the main reason this is causing upset? Is there a specific delay you're worried about?" Then, propose ideas: "Could we adjust the payment schedule to better fit your cash flow?" Turning anger into a focus on fixing the cause can build a new level of cooperation.

9.14 Handling Conflict Within a Team

Conflict is not just between you and the other side. Sometimes, your own team members disagree about the best strategy or feel their input is ignored. This can weaken your negotiating stance if your team appears disorganized.

To manage internal conflicts:

1. **Hold Pre-Meetings**: Address disagreements privately before meeting the other side.
2. **Set Clear Roles**: Assign who speaks about what topics, so people do not talk over each other.
3. **Listen to Each Member**: Make sure no one feels excluded.
4. **Agree on Key Points**: Present a united front.

A team that handles its own disputes calmly will appear more credible in the actual negotiation.

9.15 Apologizing Without Weakness

If you or your side made a mistake—maybe you missed a deadline or broke a minor promise—an apology can ease tension. But some worry that saying sorry looks weak. In fact, a sincere apology can show maturity and earn respect.

Keep it straightforward: "I apologize for the confusion. We should have sent the updated figures sooner." Then, explain how you plan to fix the issue. This approach focuses on making amends rather than dwelling on blame.

9.16 Using Objective Standards

Sometimes, conflict arises because each side has a different opinion on what is fair. You can reduce emotional arguments by pointing to objective standards, like market rates, industry norms, or official guidelines. For example, if there is a dispute about a fair price, reference a reputable cost index or a government statistic.

Objective standards help shift the debate from personal feelings to verifiable facts. This can prevent arguments from becoming too personal. If the other side sees the logic behind your position, they might be more open to compromise.

9.17 The Role of Professional Help

In some high-stakes or very tense situations, it might help to bring in a neutral party—like a mediator or an arbitrator. A mediator assists both sides in finding a path toward agreement without dictating the final result. An arbitrator, however, can make a binding decision.

When to consider outside help:

- When talks have stalled for a long time.
- When personal anger or history prevents any progress.
- When a fair process is needed to ensure both sides accept the outcome.

Though involving a third party adds complexity, it can save time and prevent further emotional damage if the negotiation has reached a dead end.

9.18 Keeping the Long-Term Relationship in Mind

If you plan to deal with the other side in the future, it is smart to limit emotional damage now. A nasty fight might end this specific deal on a sour note, making future cooperation hard. Even if you have to let go of some immediate points, preserving respect can bring benefits in the long run.

Example: A supplier that feels disrespected might start giving you poor service. A business partner who feels insulted might spread negative feedback about you in the industry. So, weigh the current conflict against your long-term interests.

9.19 Problem-Solving Steps for Conflict Resolution

When conflict is high, try a structured approach:

1. **Define the Problem**: Each side states what they see as the issue.
2. **Share Interests**: Why is this problem important to you? What do you need?
3. **Brainstorm**: List possible solutions without judging them immediately.
4. **Evaluate Options**: Pick the ideas that seem most workable.
5. **Agree on a Plan**: Finalize which solution you will try and how you will measure success.

This method keeps both parties focused on the solution rather than the drama. It also helps avoid random arguments by giving a clear set of steps to follow.

9.20 Golden Gem and Conclusion

Strong feelings can derail even the best-prepared negotiation. But these feelings do not have to destroy progress. By remaining calm, acknowledging the other side's concerns, and using techniques like short breaks or empathy, you can lower conflict. You can also turn negative feelings into a reason to explore hidden needs. This often reveals new solutions nobody saw before.

Golden gem: When tensions rise, switch from arguing to asking questions. Curiosity can replace anger by shifting focus to what the other person truly needs. This helps you discover real solutions instead of fueling a heated back-and-forth.

In the next chapter, we will talk about creative problem-solving. Handling emotions is one step toward finding inventive ideas that suit both sides. Once you can manage conflict well, you are in a strong position to explore new options and craft deals that address everyone's key concerns.

Chapter 10: Creative Problem-Solving

Negotiations often appear stuck when both sides insist on their own single solution. However, creative problem-solving can unlock fresh paths. It involves looking at a problem from many angles, considering unusual approaches, and combining smaller ideas into a better plan. By thinking in a more flexible way, you can create value that both sides appreciate.

In this chapter, we will look at how to develop solutions that go beyond the obvious. We will discuss brainstorming, exploring hidden interests, and discovering add-ons or trade-offs that can make deals more appealing. We will also show methods to test if your creative ideas will actually work in practice. By the end, you should have a toolkit of methods for turning tough standoffs into workable outcomes.

10.1 What Is Creative Problem-Solving?

Creative problem-solving is the process of finding answers beyond the standard ways. Instead of viewing a negotiation as a fixed pie—where each side simply splits resources—you look for ways to expand the options. This might mean exchanging different items of value, altering timelines, or including extra terms that fit each side's needs.

Example: In a rental negotiation, the tenant wants a lower monthly rate, but the landlord refuses. A creative option might be for the tenant to perform maintenance tasks or manage advertising for the property in exchange for a rent reduction. Both sides gain something they value.

10.2 The Power of "What If?" Questions

One of the simplest ways to spark creativity is to ask "What if?" This opens your mind to possibilities you might otherwise ignore. For example:

- What if we adjust the payment plan to match busy and slow seasons?
- What if we swap services instead of money changing hands?

- What if we bring in a third partner who can fill a gap we both have?

These questions encourage you to look past the usual patterns. You might discover a solution that satisfies key interests without requiring anyone to give up too much.

10.3 Brainstorming as a Team

In group negotiations, brainstorming can unleash many ideas. The main rule is to avoid judging ideas as soon as they appear. Let people suggest anything, even if it sounds odd initially. Later, you can filter out unrealistic options.

- **No Criticism During Brainstorming**: Negative comments stop people from sharing new thoughts.
- **Quantity Over Quality at First**: Aim for many ideas before picking the best ones.
- **Build on Each Other's Ideas**: If one suggestion sparks another, note it down.
- **Write Them All Down**: Seeing a list can help you mix and match solutions.

After the brainstorming phase, analyze which ideas are truly feasible and could meet the main needs of both sides.

10.4 Mapping Out Interests

Sometimes each side's stated position is only a partial view of what they actually need. For instance, if someone says, "I need a 15% discount," the deeper need might be, "I have a tight budget and must show cost savings to my boss." If you know that, you could suggest a smaller discount but add free shipping or other perks to show cost savings.

Steps to identify hidden interests:

1. **Ask Why**: "Why is that discount crucial?"

2. **Dig Deeper**: "Are there other ways we can help you lower costs or improve efficiency?"
3. **Listen for Emotional Needs**: Do they want respect, security, or recognition?
4. **Write Down Key Themes**: Summarize the real motivators behind their requests.

By understanding the core needs, you can craft solutions that go beyond the one thing they initially demanded.

10.5 Bundling and Packaging Deals

Sometimes you can solve disagreements by grouping several items together. For example, in a contract negotiation for office supplies, you might be stuck on the price of pens. But if you bundle pens with paper, envelopes, and toner—offering a combined rate—you might reach an overall agreement that satisfies both sides.

Advantages of bundling:

- It shifts attention from a single sticking point to a broader set of products or services.
- It allows trade-offs: maybe you agree on a lower pen price if they accept a higher price on another item.
- It creates a sense of a "package deal," which can feel more valuable.

Bundling works best when you know the other side values multiple items differently. A small concession on one item might mean a big gain on another.

10.6 Exploring Different Payment or Delivery Terms

Money is not the only form of exchange. You can explore timelines and other conditions. For instance:

- **Installment Payments**: If the buyer cannot pay one lump sum, you might arrange monthly or quarterly payments.

- **Performance-Based Payments**: If results can be measured, link payments to milestones.
- **Early Payment Discounts**: Offer a price cut if they pay sooner, which helps your cash flow.
- **Delayed Delivery**: If they cannot receive goods now, schedule a future date that benefits both sides.

Altering these variables can break a deadlock if pure price talk stalls.

10.7 Swapping Risks and Rewards

Risk-sharing is another way to be creative. If one side is worried about uncertainty—maybe future market shifts or product returns—you can balance that risk:

- **Warranties or Guarantees**: Promise to fix defects or replace items for a certain period.
- **Shared Marketing**: If both sides gain from increased sales, you might agree to promote the product together.
- **Trial Period**: Let them try a smaller order or a test run before committing fully.

By addressing risk concerns directly, you reduce their fear of loss, which might open the door to more flexible terms elsewhere.

10.8 Using Outside Resources

Sometimes, you can bring in resources from outside the two parties to expand the range of solutions:

- **Government Programs**: Grants, loans, or tax breaks that reduce financial strain.
- **Local Community or Industry Groups**: Partnerships that offer shared benefits, like joint advertising.
- **Technical Experts**: Consultants who can make the process more efficient, allowing cost savings.

When you add an outside element, new forms of value may appear, making it easier to close a deal.

10.9 Testing Feasibility Early

It is easy to get excited about a creative idea, only to find out it is not practical. Maybe it violates a law, goes beyond the budget, or requires resources neither side has. To avoid wasted effort:

1. **Check Costs**: Do a quick estimate to see if the idea is affordable.
2. **Check Timing**: Make sure the schedules for each side align with the plan.
3. **Check Stakeholder Approval**: Ask if there are higher-ups or other groups who must sign off.
4. **Check Legal or Regulatory Issues**: If the solution touches on regulated areas, ensure it is legal.

Doing a quick feasibility check early can save time and prevent disappointment later.

10.10 Shifting Perspectives

Sometimes you have to look at the problem from a completely different angle. You can do this by:

- **Role Reversal**: Pretend you are the other side. What would you want, fear, or celebrate if you were them?
- **Ask an Outsider**: Get a fresh viewpoint from someone not involved. They might see an obvious path you missed.
- **Change the Setting**: Conduct the discussion in a different environment, like a casual coffee shop instead of a formal office. This can spark new thinking.

Shifting perspectives often reveals solutions buried under standard assumptions.

10.11 Creating Options Before Deciding

A frequent error is to pick the first workable idea. While that might save time, it can lead to a less-than-ideal outcome if a better idea exists. Instead, separate the stages of "creating" options and "deciding" on them.

- **Stage 1 (Creation)**: Brainstorm and add new ideas without judging them.
- **Stage 2 (Evaluation)**: Narrow down the list to options that make sense.
- **Stage 3 (Decision)**: Pick the best idea or combine several.

This structured approach ensures you do not miss out on something more creative that could benefit everyone more.

10.12 Using Analogies and Past Successes

Sometimes, a different field has already solved a problem similar to yours. Look for analogies:

- **Sports Strategies**: Teamwork methods or ways to share resources.
- **Tech Industry**: Subscription models, free trials, or tiered pricing can be adapted elsewhere.
- **Nonprofit Operations**: They often rely on partnerships and in-kind support that might be relevant to your case.

If something worked in another context, see if you can adapt it to your negotiation. That might mean copying the basic structure, then tweaking the details to fit your needs.

10.13 Avoiding Creativity Blockers

People sometimes block creative ideas without realizing it. Phrases like "We have always done it this way" or "That would never work here" can shut down new concepts prematurely. During brainstorming or creative discussions, ban these dismissive statements. Encourage everyone to explore possibilities first, then test them.

You can also watch for your own mental blocks. If you catch yourself thinking, "That's silly," take a second to consider if there is an angle you missed. A silly-sounding idea might spark a related concept that is actually feasible.

10.14 Combining Small Ideas

Great solutions do not always come as one big breakthrough. Often, the best outcomes arise from blending several smaller ideas. For example, maybe you reduce the price a little, but in return, they accept an extended contract term, which secures your sales in the long run. At the same time, you agree to a faster delivery schedule that fits their needs.

This mix of small trade-offs can lead to a larger agreement that feels balanced. Each side gives up something minor but gains something else that is important.

10.15 Prototyping and Pilot Tests

When the negotiation involves a new product, service, or process, you can propose a "pilot" or "test run." This allows both sides to see how it works in reality without committing fully. If it goes well, you can expand. If not, you can make changes or walk away with less risk.

Benefits of pilot tests:

- **Real Feedback**: You find out what works and what doesn't in a small-scale environment.
- **Lower Risk**: Neither side invests too heavily upfront.
- **Builds Trust**: If the pilot succeeds, confidence in each other grows.

This approach can be especially useful when dealing with complex or experimental deals.

10.16 Using Mind Maps or Visual Tools

Visual tools like mind maps or flowcharts can help you see connections between issues. Start with the central problem in the middle, then branch out to related topics—cost, timeline, risk, resources. Mark sub-branches for potential solutions.

Seeing these ideas laid out can spark links you missed when thinking in a linear way. It also makes it easier to discuss possible solutions with your team or the other side. Everyone can see the bigger picture instead of focusing on a single point.

10.17 Encouraging the Other Side to Be Creative

Sometimes, the other side is not used to thinking creatively. They might only want to haggle over one factor, like price. To invite them into a more imaginative process:

1. **Ask Open-Ended Questions**: "What else would help you meet your goals?"
2. **Offer a Few Suggestions First**: Give them a sense of what creative deals could look like.
3. **Praise Their Input**: When they propose something, acknowledge the thought. This builds their confidence in sharing more ideas.
4. **Show Benefit**: Explain how creativity can help them get something they might not get through ordinary means.

If they see that flexible thinking might serve their interests, they may join you in exploring new options.

10.18 Avoiding One-Sided Creativity

Be careful not to propose solutions that heavily benefit just one side while offering little to the other. Real creativity means everyone sees value. If your ideas are clearly biased, they may view your suggestions as a trick. Instead, try to include elements that address their most pressing worries as well as yours.

For example, if you ask for a larger share of revenue, also show how your marketing support could raise total sales so they earn more too. This dual benefit approach makes your creative plan more appealing and fair.

10.19 Finalizing a Creative Deal

Once you have shaped a creative arrangement, it is time to lock in the details. Make sure:

- **All Terms Are Clear**: Write down each point—who does what, by when, and at what cost.
- **Contingencies Are Covered**: If something goes wrong, how will you handle it?
- **Both Sides Approve**: Check that everyone with authority is on board, not just the spokesperson.
- **Implementation Steps Are Outlined**: If this deal involves many parts, plan out the timeline or tasks needed.

A well-documented agreement prevents confusion later. It also helps both sides track whether the creative deal delivers the results they expected.

10.20 Golden Gem and Conclusion

Creative problem-solving can transform a deadlock into a win-win. By looking beyond standard tactics, exploring hidden needs, and trying out fresh approaches, you open doors that were shut before. The key is to stay curious and flexible, testing ideas and adjusting them until you find a fit that satisfies both parties.

Golden gem: When stuck, shift your focus from "what we cannot do" to "what we can do, even if it looks different than usual." This mental shift often sparks the biggest breakthroughs in negotiations.

In the next chapter, we will look at different approaches to bargaining (Chapter 11). While creative problem-solving is crucial, understanding the varied ways people bargain—such as making the first offer, anchoring, or using strategic concessions—will round out your skill set. Together, these techniques will help you shape deals that make sense for all involved.

Chapter 11: Approaches to Bargaining

Bargaining is often the stage in a negotiation where both sides focus on the terms of the deal—who gets what, how much is paid or received, and under what conditions. Approaches to bargaining can differ widely, based on personal style, cultural norms, or the specific context of the agreement. In this chapter, we will look at the main bargaining methods, the pros and cons of each, and the techniques used to improve your results. We will also explore concepts like anchoring, making the first offer, and how to manage concessions.

By the end of this chapter, you will see how to select the best bargaining approach for your situation. You will also know how to respond if the other side uses a particular method. Knowledge of these approaches lets you adapt and stay calm when confronted by an aggressive, collaborative, or any other style of bargainer.

11.1 Understanding Bargaining Basics

Bargaining refers to the phase where both sides exchange offers and counteroffers, looking for a final agreement. It might involve talking about prices, deadlines, or responsibilities. Even if the rest of the negotiation has gone smoothly, ineffective bargaining can spoil the outcome.

Key points in bargaining:

1. **Preparation**: If you have solid facts, clear goals, and a fallback plan, you are less likely to be pressured into a bad deal.
2. **Listening**: Understanding the other side's reasons helps you craft better offers.
3. **Flexibility**: You might need to adjust your position if it leads to a more favorable outcome overall.
4. **Respect**: Bargaining does not have to be a fight. Polite communication can keep trust levels high.

Keeping these fundamentals in mind helps you enter the bargaining stage ready to handle push-and-pull without letting things fall apart.

11.2 Common Bargaining Approaches

Different negotiators and cultures have preferred ways of bargaining. Below are a few common methods:

1. **Competitive (Win-Lose)**
    - Focus: Each side tries to get as much as possible, often at the expense of the other.
    - Typical Traits: High demands, aggressive tone, minimal sharing of information.
    - Pros: Can be effective if you only need a one-time deal and want the maximum benefit now.
    - Cons: Risks damaging relationships; can lead to mistrust.
2. **Collaborative (Win-Win)**
    - Focus: Seeks a solution that benefits both sides fairly.
    - Typical Traits: Sharing information, looking for creative ways to add value, emphasizing common goals.
    - Pros: Builds stronger ties and can lead to repeated partnerships.
    - Cons: Requires both sides to be cooperative, which is not always the case.
3. **Compromise**
    - Focus: Each side gives up something to reach a middle ground quickly.
    - Typical Traits: Aim for a moderate solution; often used when time is short.
    - Pros: Good for resolving simple disputes without too much back-and-forth.
    - Cons: Might overlook better solutions; each side might feel partially dissatisfied.
4. **Avoidance**
    - Focus: Not engaging deeply, hoping the issue resolves itself or is postponed.

- Typical Traits: Evasive answers, delayed meetings, or ignoring the problem.
- Pros: Can be a short-term relief if the issue is minor or if emotions are high.
- Cons: Often creates bigger issues later and can cause confusion.

5. **Accommodation**
    - Focus: One side yields more to maintain harmony or build goodwill.
    - Typical Traits: Quick agreement to the other side's demands.
    - Pros: May be useful if preserving the relationship is top priority.
    - Cons: Can lead to resentment or a loss of resources.

No single method is always best. The right approach depends on factors like time, the importance of the relationship, and how much each side values specific outcomes.

11.3 Making the First Offer: Pros and Cons

A well-known discussion in bargaining is whether you should make the first offer or let the other side speak first. This decision can set the tone for the entire process.

- **Advantages of Making the First Offer**:
    1. **Anchoring**: You set a reference point for all future talk.
    2. **Shows Preparedness**: A confident first offer backed by data can make the other side take you seriously.
    3. **Directional Control**: You steer the conversation around your figures.
- **Disadvantages of Making the First Offer**:
    1. **Insufficient Information**: If you do not fully understand the other side's position, your first offer might be too high or too low.
    2. **Risk of Overreach**: A number that is too aggressive can offend or scare them away.

3. **Possibility of Missing a Better Deal**: The other side might have been willing to offer more or accept less.

If you have done thorough research and have a solid sense of the market or the other side's constraints, making the first offer can help you shape the negotiation. However, if you are unsure of their needs, letting them speak first might reveal more about their expectations.

11.4 Anchoring: How It Influences Outcomes

Anchoring involves establishing an initial reference point—usually a price or quantity—from which the discussion proceeds. For instance, if you say, "We would like to sell at $10 per unit," the conversation will likely revolve around that figure. The other side might say $8 or $9, but rarely $2 or $15, because your anchor plants an idea of a "normal range."

Effective anchoring tips:

- Use a precise figure rather than a round number. It implies you have done detailed calculations.
- Back your anchor with reasons or data. That makes it harder for the other side to dismiss it.
- Watch out for their anchors. If they anchor first, counter with data that supports your own reference point, rather than simply moving a little in their direction.

Anchoring can be powerful but be careful not to pick an extreme number that appears unrealistic, which might damage trust or cause them to end talks.

11.5 Concession Strategies

Concessions are the trade-offs you make during bargaining. You might lower your price, offer an extra feature, or agree to a shorter timeline. Concessions are normal in negotiations, but how you handle them matters.

1. **Plan Your Concessions in Advance**: Decide which points you can give up easily and which are essential.
2. **Never Give Without Getting**: If you concede on something major, ask for something in return.
3. **Concede Slowly**: Do not rush to give away too much. If you give too many concessions quickly, the other side may expect more.
4. **Signal Finality**: When you reach a point where you cannot give more, state it clearly.

Concessions help move from deadlock to agreement, but they should be done thoughtfully to protect your interests while respecting the other side's needs.

11.6 Patterns of Bargaining: Hard vs. Soft

Some negotiators take a "hard" approach, pushing aggressively, showing little flexibility, and often threatening to leave if they do not get their way. Others take a "soft" approach, showing willingness to compromise early, focusing on preserving harmony.

- **Hard Approach Advantages**: You may gain more in the short term if the other side fears losing the deal.
- **Hard Approach Disadvantages**: You risk angering them or losing future opportunities.
- **Soft Approach Advantages**: Fosters goodwill, can lead to longer-term partnerships.
- **Soft Approach Disadvantages**: You might be taken advantage of by a more forceful negotiator.

A balanced approach—sometimes called "principled" or "firm but fair"—can combine the clarity and persistence of a hard style with the empathy and respect of a soft style.

11.7 Timing in Bargaining

Timing can dramatically affect the outcome. Even if your offer is good, presenting it at the wrong moment can diminish its impact. Conversely, a carefully timed concession can build momentum toward a final agreement.

1. **Early Bargaining**: You might set a strong anchor or gather information.
2. **Mid-Bargaining**: This is often where core trades happen. Being patient can yield useful insights about the other side's limits.
3. **Final Stage**: Deadlines, real or perceived, can push people to close deals. Some negotiators hold back their best offer until near the end.

Try not to show desperation as a deadline approaches. If they sense you must make a deal urgently, they may press you for deeper concessions.

11.8 Handling Tough Bargainers

Some people use intimidating tactics, from making personal remarks to setting artificial deadlines. Here are ways to handle them:

- **Stay Calm**: Do not mirror their aggression. Keep your composure.
- **Ask Clarifying Questions**: If they throw out a threat, ask them to explain it, which can reduce its emotional power.
- **Focus on Principles**: Refer back to market norms, data, or shared interests to bring the talk back to facts.
- **Consider Walking Away**: If the other side is truly unreasonable or uses unethical methods, it might be best to end the negotiation.

Tough bargainers often rely on pushing emotional buttons. By staying grounded and highlighting logic, you can neutralize much of their impact.

11.9 Working Toward a Collaborative Style

If you aim for a lasting relationship, a collaborative approach can yield better overall results. Collaborative bargaining involves:

1. **Transparency of Interests**: Both sides share what they actually want, not just positions.
2. **Creative Idea Generation**: Instead of only splitting the difference, look for ways to add value.
3. **Joint Problem-Solving**: "We want X, you want Y—how can we arrange resources so we both benefit?"
4. **Maintaining Respect**: Even if you disagree, you keep communication constructive.

Collaboration works best when the other side is also open to it. If they remain combative, you may need to adjust your strategy.

11.10 Bridging Differences

Sometimes, two sides have positions that are far apart. They seem to want opposite things. Bridging that gap may require a mediator, or at least a neutral set of facts everyone trusts—like a public price index or an industry standard. If the gap is too wide, you may try a gradual approach: start with less sensitive areas where agreement is easier, build trust there, then move to bigger points.

Bridge-Building Steps:

- **Find Common Ground**: Identify any shared goals, such as quality standards or timely delivery.
- **Set Low-Stakes Agreements First**: Solve smaller items to build momentum.
- **Use a "Trial" Agreement**: If you cannot find a permanent deal yet, try a short-term arrangement to see how both sides work together.

This method reduces the feeling of an "all or nothing" standoff.

11.11 Documenting and Reviewing Offers

During bargaining, it is easy to lose track of who said what. Keeping notes is very helpful:

- **List All Offers**: Write down each offer and counteroffer with dates.
- **Highlight Concessions**: Note what you gave up and what you got in return.
- **Mark Tentative Agreements**: If both sides agree on a point, mark it as settled to avoid rearguing it.
- **Track Deadlines**: Some offers expire or need action by a certain date.

Reviewing your notes before each new round helps you avoid confusion and maintain a cohesive strategy.

11.12 Final Check Before Closing the Deal

As the bargaining stage nears its end, do not rush to sign before a final review. Make sure:

1. **All Major Points Are Covered**: Price, deadlines, responsibilities, warranties, etc.
2. **No Hidden Surprises**: Check for unclear language or contradictory clauses.
3. **Confirm Agreement with Key Decision-Makers**: Ensure the people who hold actual authority on both sides have given approval.
4. **Review the Relationship Impact**: If you plan to continue working together, confirm that the deal fosters mutual respect.

Taking a moment to confirm each detail can prevent costly mistakes or misunderstandings.

11.13 Examples of Bargaining Scenarios

1. **Salary Negotiation**: You might anchor with a desired salary figure, the boss counters, and you discuss benefits, bonuses, or flexible hours. Concessions can come in the form of more paid time off versus a smaller raise, for instance.
2. **Supplier and Manufacturer**: A supplier wants to maintain their prices; the manufacturer wants a discount. They might compromise by agreeing to a slightly lower price but for a longer contract term.
3. **Team Project Disputes**: Team members might bargain over who handles which tasks. A solution could involve exchanging responsibilities so each member focuses on their strengths.

These examples show how bargaining can apply in various settings, from professional to personal life.

11.14 Pitfalls in Bargaining

1. **Overlooking Non-Monetary Factors**: Only focusing on price can miss out on other beneficial terms, like deadlines or services.
2. **Rushing**: Jumping to a conclusion out of impatience can lead to missing better options.
3. **Emotional Traps**: Letting anger or pride drive your decisions rather than logic and fairness.
4. **Rigid Positions**: Refusing to adapt or explore alternatives might cause a deal to collapse.

Being aware of these pitfalls helps you stay flexible and level-headed during crucial talks.

11.15 Balancing Short-Term Wins and Long-Term Relationships

Sometimes you can push hard and extract a better immediate deal, but this might damage trust if the other side feels taken advantage of. In contrast, a balanced deal that leaves both sides relatively satisfied can lead to repeated business or good references in the future.

Ask yourself: "Is it worth gaining a little extra now if it risks losing this relationship entirely?" The answer might vary depending on whether you value future collaboration or if this is a one-time transaction. Knowing your priorities helps you pick the right bargaining style.

11.16 Cultural Aspects of Bargaining

Cultures differ in how they view direct confrontation, personal space, decision speed, and level of formality. In some places, bargaining is expected and may even include raised voices or strong gestures without ill intent. In others, a more reserved approach is common.

If you are dealing across cultures, do some research. Adapting slightly to their norms can prevent misunderstandings or accidental insults. We will explore cultural differences in greater detail in Chapter 12, but keep in mind that style preferences can deeply affect bargaining talks.

11.17 Handling Stalemates

A stalemate occurs when both sides feel stuck. Neither wants to concede further. Possible ways to break a stalemate include:

1. **Introduce a Neutral Party**: A mediator might suggest new angles.
2. **Change the Setting**: Move to a different location or switch from email to a face-to-face meeting.
3. **Revisit Shared Goals**: Remind each other of what you both want to achieve.
4. **Park the Tough Issue**: Temporarily set aside the hardest point and agree on others first. Sometimes progress elsewhere can unlock new ideas.

Understanding that stalemates are common can help you remain calm and patient until you find a breakthrough.

11.18 Ethical Considerations

Ethics in bargaining means you should not lie about essential facts or use manipulative tactics that cross moral lines. While you do not have to reveal everything, blatant dishonesty erodes trust. You can be assertive without being unethical. Respect for both sides' dignity and a fair mindset will keep your reputation strong.

If you suspect the other side is using unethical methods—like hiding critical safety details or forging data—you may need to confront it or walk away for your own protection. A short-term gain is not worth a long-term hit to your moral standards or potential legal trouble.

11.19 When to End Negotiations

Sometimes, despite all efforts, a deal is not possible. Perhaps the gaps in price, goals, or timelines are too large, or the other side remains hostile. Walking away is an option if:

- The final terms do not meet your essential needs.
- The other side breaks trust through dishonesty.
- The cost of continuing is higher than what you might gain.
- You have a better alternative (your backup plan is more attractive).

Ending talks respectfully, without burning bridges, keeps open the possibility of future discussions if conditions change.

11.20 Golden Gem and Conclusion

Bargaining is where the negotiation's ideas become specific commitments. Approaches can range from tough and competitive to open and cooperative. Understanding anchoring, concession tactics, timing, and cultural factors helps you steer through these discussions with more confidence. Keep in mind the relationship aspect—sometimes preserving goodwill matters just as much as the numbers on the page.

Golden gem: Concessions should feel like a meaningful exchange, not a surrender. Each time you give up something, ensure you gain a fair benefit in return. This practice helps maintain balance, trust, and a sense of mutual respect in the final outcome.

In the next chapter, we will focus on cultural differences in negotiation (Chapter 12). Cultural values can shape bargaining behaviors, communication styles, and expectations of fairness. By learning how to adapt to various cultural norms, you can avoid missteps and foster smoother discussions, no matter where you do business or interact with others.

Chapter 12: Understanding Cultural Differences

In an increasingly connected world, it is common to negotiate with people from diverse cultures. Culture can influence views on hierarchy, time, communication style, and the importance of relationships. A tactic that works well in one culture may seem offensive or ineffective in another. Recognizing these cultural nuances can help avoid misunderstandings and establish a more respectful environment.

This chapter will explain how cultural backgrounds affect negotiation behavior. We will look at concepts like power distance, individualism vs. group focus, direct vs. indirect communication, and attitudes toward punctuality. We will also share tips on adapting your style without losing your identity. By the end, you will be better prepared to handle cross-cultural talks with sensitivity and skill.

12.1 What Is Culture?

Culture is the shared set of values, beliefs, traditions, behaviors, and norms that shape how a group of people interact. It is passed down through generations and affects daily life—how people greet each other, how decisions are made, and what is considered polite or rude.

Examples of Cultural Influences:

- In some countries, calling a senior manager by their first name might be seen as too casual or disrespectful.
- In other places, direct eye contact is a sign of respect, while in some cultures it might be considered too bold.
- Some groups expect a small gift when meeting, while others see gift-giving as potential bribery.

Understanding these differences does not mean stereotyping; rather, it means being aware of possible variations in behavior so you can adjust or clarify when needed.

12.2 High-Context vs. Low-Context Cultures

Anthropologist Edward T. Hall introduced the idea of high-context and low-context communication:

- **High-Context Cultures** (e.g., many parts of Asia, the Middle East, and Latin America):
    - Communication relies heavily on context, body language, relationships, and unspoken cues.
    - People often speak indirectly and expect listeners to read between the lines.
    - Direct criticism can be seen as too blunt or disrespectful.
- **Low-Context Cultures** (e.g., the United States, Germany, Northern Europe):
    - Communication is more direct, with clear, explicit statements.
    - People value straightforwardness and clarity.
    - Indirect hints might confuse them because they expect you to say exactly what you mean.

Knowing whether you are dealing with a high or low-context culture helps you adjust your style. In a high-context setting, pay attention to subtler signals. In a low-context setting, be explicit and clear.

12.3 Individualism vs. Group Focus

Another cultural factor is whether a society leans more toward individualism or group-focused values:

- **Individualist Cultures** (e.g., the United States, Australia, many Western nations):
    - Personal goals and individual rights are highly valued.
    - Negotiators may focus on personal gain or company profit.
    - Decisions can be made by individuals with authority.

- **Group-Focused Cultures** (e.g., Japan, China, many African and Latin American societies):
    - The group's or community's needs are prioritized.
    - Preserving harmony and relationships can overshadow direct profit.
    - Decisions might require group consensus or approval from elders or senior figures.

If you are negotiating in a group-focused culture, pushing individual advantage too strongly can be off-putting. Instead, emphasize how the deal benefits the entire team or community. In an individualist culture, presenting a clear personal or corporate advantage might resonate more.

12.4 Power Distance

Power distance refers to how much a culture accepts unequal distribution of power:

- **High Power Distance** (e.g., many Asian, Middle Eastern, and Latin American nations):
    - People respect authority and hierarchies.
    - Junior members may not openly challenge or question senior leaders.
    - Formal titles and respectful greetings are common.
- **Low Power Distance** (e.g., Scandinavia, the Netherlands, some Western countries):
    - Roles are more equal, with less rigid hierarchy.
    - Junior members can speak freely and challenge senior leaders if needed.
    - Casual interactions with bosses or senior figures are normal.

If you come from a low power distance culture and meet a high power distance counterpart, pushing for an informal, equal style could cause discomfort or seem disrespectful. Conversely, if you are used to high power distance and find yourself in a low power distance setting, overly formal behavior might seem stiff or overly deferential.

12.5 Attitudes Toward Time

Time perception also varies. Some cultures operate on strict schedules (often called "monochronic"), while others are more flexible ("polychronic"):

- **Monochronic Cultures** (e.g., Germany, Switzerland, the U.S. in many cases):
    - Punctuality is crucial.
    - Meetings start and end at set times.
    - People usually tackle one task at a time.
- **Polychronic Cultures** (e.g., many Middle Eastern and Latin American regions):
    - Being a bit late might not be a big deal.
    - Several conversations or tasks can happen at once.
    - Relationship-building can take precedence over rigid scheduling.

When scheduling meetings across these differences, be patient if someone does not arrive exactly on time in a polychronic culture. Conversely, if dealing with a monochronic partner, try to be prompt or let them know if you will be late.

12.6 Formal vs. Informal Communication

Some cultures prefer formality in greetings, titles, and dress code. Others are more relaxed. Formal cultures may expect you to use proper titles (Mr., Ms., Dr.) and dress conservatively. Informal cultures might be fine calling each other by first names after a short introduction.

You can usually observe cues. If they greet you using your title, consider returning the courtesy. If they dress formally, match that level of professionalism. Adapting to local customs shows respect and can make your counterpart feel at ease.

12.7 Building Relationships

In some places, it is normal to spend a lot of time building a relationship before talking business. Sharing a meal, personal stories, or small gifts might be a way to show trust and sincerity. In other cultures, people prefer to get straight to the point and may see lengthy social talk as irrelevant.

Tips for relationship-building in different cultures:

- **If they expect social time**, do not rush into business talk. Accept invitations to lunch or casual chats.
- **If they prefer directness**, keep small talk brief and move to the main topic.
- **Ask about local etiquette**: For instance, do you wait for the host to bring up business, or is it okay to mention it first?

Finding the right balance can greatly enhance the negotiation mood.

12.8 Communication Style: Direct vs. Indirect

As touched on earlier, some cultures are direct. They say "No" if they disagree. Others are indirect, using phrases like "We will think about it," which might mean "No." If you come from a direct culture and you hear "We will consider it," you might think they are open to the idea when they are actually rejecting it politely.

Likewise, if you are from an indirect culture, simply saying "No" might seem too blunt. You could use softer expressions, but the other side (from a direct culture) might miss the hint. Clarifying language is key. If you sense confusion, do not be afraid to say, "I want to confirm: should I interpret your statement as a yes or as a no to this proposal?"

12.9 Saving Face

In certain cultures, the concept of "face" is very important. Losing face can mean losing respect or feeling publicly embarrassed. People might avoid saying something that makes another person look bad in front of others. They may also find indirect ways to express disagreement or dissatisfaction to preserve harmony.

If saving face is critical in the other side's culture:

1. **Offer Criticism Privately**: Do not call them out or correct them harshly in front of their peers.
2. **Use Gentle Language**: Instead of saying, "That is wrong," say, "Could we consider a different approach?"
3. **Allow Them a Dignified Way Out**: If they need to backtrack on a statement, do not rub it in. Let them save face by focusing on solutions rather than blame.

Recognizing the importance of face can prevent hurt feelings and keep negotiations positive.

12.10 Negotiating Styles Across Cultures

Different cultures may lean toward different bargaining approaches:

- **Some East Asian cultures**: Often emphasize harmony and indirect communication; building trust might be a longer process.
- **Mediterranean cultures**: May use passionate gestures and discussions, sometimes appearing heated even if the relationship is friendly.
- **Northern European cultures**: Tend to be straightforward, with minimal small talk. They might value logic and efficiency.
- **Latin American cultures**: Relationship-building can be crucial, with flexible time. Meetings may start later, but personal bonds can be strong.

These are broad generalizations, so never assume every individual in a culture behaves identically. Still, being aware can guide your initial approach.

12.11 Religion and Ethical Views

Religion can also shape negotiation styles, influencing honesty, fairness, and forms of greeting. In some regions, prayer or religious references might be common in business settings. Or certain foods or beverages might be avoided at meetings.

If religion could affect your discussions:

- **Be Informed**: Know basic do's and don'ts (e.g., dietary restrictions, religious holidays).
- **Respect Boundaries**: Ask politely if you are unsure about a custom.
- **Avoid Controversial Topics**: Unless they bring it up, steer clear of disagreements about religious doctrines.

Showing respect for their beliefs fosters trust, even if your own beliefs differ.

12.12 Gift-Giving Practices

In some societies, gift-giving is a normal part of building goodwill. In others, it may be seen as bribery or create a conflict of interest. The rules can be subtle. For example, in certain cultures, a modest gift with a company logo is acceptable, but an expensive personal item might be frowned upon.

When unsure:

1. **Ask for Advice**: If you have local contacts, ask them what is appropriate.
2. **Choose Symbolic Gifts**: Items that represent your home region or company brand but are not lavish.
3. **Follow Official Policies**: Some businesses have strict rules on accepting gifts above a certain value.

Gifts can be a way to show respect or gratitude, but only if they align with local norms.

12.13 Pacing and Decision-Making

Cultures also vary in how they reach decisions. In some places, one person (often the highest in rank) makes the call. In others, consensus is important, and many people must be consulted. Negotiations might take longer, with multiple rounds of internal discussion.

Tips for adapting:

- **If they need consensus**, expect possible delays while they consult team members.
- **If a single leader decides**, direct crucial points to that leader but do not ignore others—they might still influence the leader.
- **Ask about their process**: Politely inquire, "How does your team usually reach final approval?" so you can adjust expectations.

Patience is key. If you push too hard for a quick conclusion in a culture that values group agreement, you might seem insensitive or suspicious.

12.14 Conflict Resolution Across Cultures

When conflict arises, different cultures have preferred resolution methods. Some might prefer direct confrontation, while others prefer mediation or quietly working things out behind the scenes. In group-focused cultures, personal conflicts might be seen as a threat to overall harmony, so they try to handle it discreetly.

If you see a conflict looming:

- **Observe Their Style**: Do they bring it up openly or hint at it indirectly?
- **Suggest Solutions Carefully**: Maybe propose a mediator if that fits their norms.
- **Avoid Shaming**: Focus on solving the issue, not blaming individuals.

Adjusting to their conflict style can prevent disagreements from escalating.

12.15 Technology in Cross-Cultural Negotiations

Emails and video calls can complicate cultural nuances. In a high-context culture, subtle nonverbal cues are often missing in an email. Words may be interpreted differently without tone or facial expressions. A direct statement that seems normal to a low-context negotiator may appear rude to a high-context reader.

To handle this:

1. **Use Video Conferencing When Possible**: At least some visual cues can be seen.
2. **Be Polite and Clear in Writing**: Avoid abbreviations or slang they might not recognize.
3. **Confirm Understanding**: Invite them to ask questions or clarify any part of your message.

Remember that time zone differences can also affect response times and scheduling.

12.16 Overcoming Stereotypes

While cultural awareness is helpful, beware of stereotyping. Not everyone from a certain culture behaves the same way. Personal upbringing, education, and individual personality also matter. The best approach is to see cultural guidelines as clues, not as fixed rules.

Ways to avoid harmful stereotypes:

- **Stay Curious**: Ask questions about their preferences and experiences instead of assuming.
- **Notice Individual Behaviors**: Watch how the specific person acts rather than relying on generalizations.
- **Keep an Open Mind**: Adapt if you see them using a style different from what you expected.

Balancing cultural knowledge with genuine respect for personal differences leads to better outcomes.

12.17 Learning Basic Local Phrases

In many places, showing effort to speak a bit of the local language can build rapport. Even simple greetings or "thank you" can show respect. However, do not overdo it or mispronounce phrases to the point where it becomes awkward. A small, sincere attempt is usually appreciated.

If the negotiation is high-stakes and language is a big barrier, consider hiring an interpreter. A professional interpreter can ensure clarity, especially if the other side's English (or your language) is limited. But keep eye contact with the other party, not just the interpreter, to maintain a direct personal connection.

12.18 Handling Business Cards and Titles

In some Asian cultures, for instance, giving and receiving business cards is almost ceremonial. You may be expected to present it with both hands, read it carefully, and then put it in a holder rather than shoving it in your pocket. Failing to do so can seem rude.

Also, using titles properly can matter. If the other person has "Professor," "Doctor," or another honorific, use it until they invite you to do otherwise. This shows you acknowledge their status or achievement.

12.19 Example Scenarios of Cultural Nuances

1. **Negotiating in Japan**
    - High-context environment.
    - Expect more silence during talks—silence can show thoughtfulness.

- Bowing is a common greeting; wait for cues to see how low you should bow.
2. **Negotiating in the United States**
   - Low-context environment, direct communication is standard.
   - Time is money; tardiness can leave a negative impression.
   - Titles matter less; first names are often used quickly.
3. **Negotiating in Brazil**
   - Personal relationships and informal chat are important.
   - Expect flexible scheduling; meetings can start later.
   - Warm body language and closer personal space might be normal.

By understanding these norms in broad terms, you can avoid unintentional rudeness and adapt to local styles.

12.20 Golden Gem and Conclusion

Negotiating across cultures can be both challenging and rewarding. Cultural differences affect how people communicate, handle time, show respect, and view authority. By learning about these factors, you reduce the chances of misunderstanding and increase the likelihood of a respectful, productive discussion.

Golden gem: When unsure about cultural etiquette, politely ask or observe what others do. Showing a willingness to learn is often more appreciated than pretending you know it all.

In the next chapter, we will explore negotiations in business settings (Chapter 13). Whether you are closing sales deals, forming partnerships, or managing internal contracts, an awareness of cultural nuances can be a huge asset, especially in today's global market.

Chapter 13: Negotiations in Business

Business negotiations happen in many forms. Companies negotiate deals with suppliers, employees negotiate salaries with their bosses, and service providers discuss prices with clients. In each scenario, the ability to negotiate well can shape profits, career growth, or the stability of a partnership. This chapter examines the nature of negotiations in the business world, highlighting strategies for different types of deals, the importance of data and relationships, and ways to address common pitfalls. By understanding these concepts, you can handle business talks more confidently and protect your interests while building better professional connections.

13.1 The Range of Business Negotiations

Business negotiations can vary widely in scope:

1. **Contract Talks**: Companies often discuss terms with vendors or service providers. This might include payment timelines, product specifications, or conflict-resolution clauses.
2. **Salary and Compensation**: Workers frequently negotiate pay, bonuses, health benefits, or remote-work arrangements.
3. **Mergers and Acquisitions**: Large-scale talks where one company purchases or merges with another, often involving complex legal and financial terms.
4. **Joint Ventures**: Two or more organizations form a partnership to pursue a shared project or goal.
5. **Sales Deals**: A firm might sell products or services to another business or directly to consumers. The final price and terms can be subject to negotiation.
6. **Licensing and Royalties**: Creative or technical work might be licensed for a fee or royalty, with the specifics requiring careful discussion.

Though details differ, many principles remain the same: clarity, preparation, fairness, and adaptability. Still, business talks can have higher stakes, involving larger sums of money or official contracts. These factors bring extra pressure, making it vital to approach such negotiations with thorough research and a clear plan.

13.2 Research as a Business Necessity

In business contexts, poor research can lead to major losses. Before entering discussions, gather as much data as possible:

- **Market Rates**: If it is a salary conversation or a product sale, know the standard ranges. If your number is too high above the norm, potential partners might refuse to continue. If it is too low, you miss revenue.
- **Financial Health of the Other Side**: Public companies publish financial reports, allowing you to see their revenue, profit, or areas of cost-cutting. If a firm is struggling, they might push harder for lower prices. If they are thriving, they might have more room to accept higher fees if value is demonstrated.
- **Trends and Competition**: Keep track of what others in the same market are doing. If your competition offers faster shipping, it might matter in your talks.
- **Legal Constraints**: Business regulations differ by location or industry. Make sure you know any rules about minimum wages, data protection, or mandatory insurance.

Having a solid foundation of facts and figures not only boosts your confidence but also acts as a shield against extreme demands. If you can cite a known industry survey or a reliable economic statistic, the other side is less likely to reject your figures.

13.3 Building Business Relationships

While facts matter, relationships can be just as critical in business negotiations. If you plan to deal with the same party repeatedly—such as a supplier you reorder from every year—invest in rapport. Show reliability by following through on small promises, like sending documents on time or responding politely to their questions.

- **Regular Communication**: A quick message updating them on your progress can build trust.
- **Respect Their Schedule**: If they work in a different time zone or have busy seasons, plan your talks thoughtfully.
- **Add Small Courtesies**: Simple gestures like thanking them for their time or offering to adapt meeting times can foster goodwill.

These actions show you value them, which can result in more flexibility when you negotiate. If a relationship is strong, the other side may be more willing to consider solutions that help you both. On the other hand, neglecting the human aspect and focusing only on numbers can make a negotiation feel cold, causing tension over small points.

13.4 Handling Contract Details

Contracts are a hallmark of business agreements. They define roles, responsibilities, payment terms, timelines, and potential remedies if something goes wrong. When negotiating contracts:

1. **Know the Key Clauses**: Common sections include scope of work, payment schedule, warranties, and dispute resolution processes.
2. **Identify Must-Haves**: For instance, you may need a clear clause about intellectual property ownership, or an exit clause if a project stalls.
3. **Anticipate Problems**: Think about worst-case scenarios. If the shipment is late, how is that addressed? If a vendor's product fails quality checks, what happens next?
4. **Seek Legal Help if Needed**: For complex deals, an attorney can ensure all wording is correct and that you do not accept hidden risks.

A contract is a safety net that reduces ambiguity. It forces each side to articulate expectations clearly, which prevents many disputes down the line. However, drafting or reviewing them can be time-consuming, so plan accordingly.

13.5 Salary and Compensation Negotiations

For individual workers, one of the most critical business discussions is salary and benefits. Whether you are applying for a new job or seeking a raise at your current position, the steps include:

- **Assess Your Value**: Examine market data for similar roles, your experience, and recent accomplishments.
- **Set a Range**: Know your ideal figure and a lower bound you can accept if the role has other perks.
- **Highlight Achievements**: Show your ability to boost the company's bottom line, solve problems, or improve operations.
- **Consider Non-Monetary Perks**: Sometimes, if the salary cannot go higher, you can negotiate more vacation days, flexible hours, or professional development funds.

Remain polite but confident. Most employers expect a bit of negotiation, so politely stating your research-based request is normal. If they cannot meet your number, see if there is a midpoint or a step increase over time. Keep the discussion factual, referencing industry norms and your proven results, to avoid emotional tension.

13.6 Sales and Client Negotiations

Companies that sell products or services often face regular bargaining with customers or clients. You need to find a price that customers see as fair while keeping enough profit for your business. Key points:

1. **Value Proposition**: Emphasize what sets your offering apart. If you charge more, explain why—maybe better quality, brand prestige, or superior support.
2. **Discount Strategies**: Decide in advance how much discount you can allow and under what conditions (bulk orders, off-season deals, etc.).

3. **Customer Relationship**: A demanding client might consistently negotiate a lower price. Is the volume they purchase worth it? Could you find a replacement client who pays more?
4. **Upselling and Bundles**: Instead of lowering the price, add extra features or bundle services to justify your rate.

Sometimes, you might face a client who claims they can get the same product cheaper elsewhere. If you have data showing your quality is higher or your support is better, present it. Be ready to match certain price points or walk away if it is not profitable.

13.7 Internal Negotiations

Negotiations within a single organization can be less formal, but they still matter. Departments might compete for budget allocations or debate timelines for shared projects. Common internal talks include:

- **Resource Allocation**: Which team gets more staffing, equipment, or software licenses?
- **Workflow Scheduling**: A production team might want more time to ensure quality, while a sales team pushes for faster delivery.
- **Policy Changes**: Updates to work policies or procedures might require consensus or trade-offs.

Even though you all work for the same company, each department has distinct goals. Approach these talks with a mindset of collaboration. Show how your request serves the broader mission of the business. If a colleague is reluctant, ask about their worries and see if you can address them.

13.8 Power Dynamics in Business

Unlike personal or informal settings, a business context may present power imbalances:

- **Large vs. Small Company**: A major corporation can push stricter terms on a tiny supplier due to its massive purchasing power.

- **Employer vs. Employee**: A boss has the ability to hire or fire, giving them leverage in pay talks.
- **Exclusive Intellectual Property**: If one side owns a patented technology, they might have a monopoly on it, increasing their power.

To manage such imbalances, highlight unique strengths you bring. A small firm might offer personalized service or faster decision-making. An employee might bring rare skills or a track record of critical achievements. While you might not erase the power gap, you can show why the other side benefits from accommodating you.

13.9 The Role of Emotions in Business Deals

Emotions are present in business as well, even if people expect more formal behavior. A stressed manager might give in too quickly, or an overconfident executive might push a risky demand. Recognizing emotional triggers and staying calm can prevent hasty mistakes. If tempers rise in a business meeting, suggest a short break or shift focus to a less contentious topic for a while.

Also, be aware of the other party's emotional cues. If you sense frustration, clarify points to ensure you are not creating misunderstandings. Show empathy where appropriate—"I see why the timeline is tight for you"—and then propose possible solutions. Balancing professionalism with a degree of human understanding often leads to better outcomes.

13.10 Time Considerations and Deadlines

Business discussions sometimes operate under strict deadlines: a product must launch before a holiday, or a budget review is scheduled next week. These constraints can influence bargaining strategies:

- **Use of Deadlines**: If you know the other side has to decide soon, you might stand firm on your price. On the other hand, if you are

the one facing a firm date, they might press you for more concessions.
- **Phased Agreements**: When time is short, sometimes you can settle major terms quickly and agree to refine minor details later.
- **Avoid Last-Second Panic**: Try not to let deadlines force you into poorly considered deals. If possible, prepare a backup plan so you do not appear desperate.

Time is a tool in negotiations, but it can also be a trap if you fail to plan. Keep track of milestones and alert the other party in advance if you foresee delays.

13.11 Understanding Industry Practices

Some business negotiations follow industry-specific customs. For example, in construction contracting, it is common to include penalty clauses if a project is not finished on schedule. In technology licensing, royalty rates might be set at standard percentages. Doing your homework on these norms helps you avoid making demands that seem out of place.

Also, some industries have associations or trade groups that publish guidelines or recommended contract templates. Using these as a reference can speed up talks and reduce friction, since both sides recognize them as standard practices.

13.12 Handling International Business Deals

International negotiations add complexity because of differences in legal systems, currencies, and cultural expectations. As discussed in Chapter 12, you must understand cultural nuances like communication style or power distance. You also need to:

- **Learn Basic Legal Requirements**: Import taxes, tariffs, or foreign investment rules might shape your agreement.

- **Agree on a Governing Law and Venue**: If a dispute occurs, which country's courts will handle it? This point should be in the contract.
- **Currency Fluctuations**: If payments are made in another currency, consider how exchange rates might shift over the contract period. Some deals include clauses adjusting prices if currency swings become large.

Being aware of these factors reduces surprises. You might also consider hiring local advisors if the country's regulations are unfamiliar.

13.13 Ethics and Reputation

Ethical lapses in business can lead to serious consequences—fines, legal actions, or public backlash. Negotiations must respect legal boundaries. Misrepresenting your finances, promising more than you can deliver, or hiding safety issues can damage your reputation. Honest communication is critical for maintaining goodwill.

- **Transparency vs. Tactics**: You do not have to reveal every detail of your strategy, but do not lie about basic facts.
- **Respect Fair Competition**: Some industries have rules against collusion or price-fixing. Be aware of antitrust laws.
- **Build a Long-Term View**: A single unethical deal might bring short-term gains but destroy trust in future deals.

When you handle talks ethically, you set a positive tone that can differentiate you in a competitive marketplace.

13.14 Negotiating in High-Pressure Sales

Some business contexts involve fast-paced transactions with heavy pressure—like buying or selling real estate or large equipment. A salesperson might say, "If you do not sign now, the offer expires." If you are on the receiving end, remain cautious. High pressure can cause rushed decisions. If you need more time to evaluate, say so. Suggest you would like to confirm funding or compare other quotes.

If you are the seller, be wary of pushing too hard. You might scare away potential customers who feel cornered. Balancing urgency with respect for the buyer's decision process often leads to a more stable deal. Repeat or returning customers can be more profitable than one-time sales gained through aggressive tactics.

13.15 Virtual Negotiations in Business

Many business talks now happen online. While video calls and emails are convenient, they reduce face-to-face interaction. To adapt:

1. **Test Technology**: Make sure your connection, microphone, and camera work well. Technical problems disrupt serious talks.
2. **Clarity in Writing**: When you send proposals by email, be precise about terms. Avoid vague statements.
3. **Schedule Appropriately**: Time zones might be an issue if you are dealing with international partners. Find slots that are fair to all.
4. **Watch Tone**: Digital communication can come across as cold or blunt. Use polite language and consider short calls to confirm important details rather than sending only text-based updates.

Though virtual methods save travel and time, they also remove some nonverbal cues. Use direct yet respectful communication to avoid misunderstandings.

13.16 Conflict Resolution in Business Deals

Disagreements can arise over missed deadlines, faulty products, or unexpected costs. When a business conflict appears, try:

- **Direct Discussion**: See if you can resolve it informally by phone or in person.

- **Mediation**: A neutral third party may help clarify each side's concerns and suggest compromise.
- **Arbitration or Legal Routes**: If the contract mandates arbitration, you present your case to a chosen arbitrator. Court is usually a last resort, given its cost and time.
- **Preserve the Relationship**: If future business is valuable, avoid letting anger dominate. Seek a resolution that might keep the door open for further collaboration.

Acknowledging mistakes—if you made one—and proposing how to fix them can show good faith. Many times, the other side appreciates honesty and might be more open to a fair settlement.

13.17 Using Data and Analytics

Modern businesses often rely on analytics. From tracking consumer behavior online to monitoring operational metrics, you can use data to strengthen your negotiation stance. For example:

- **Pricing Models**: Show how a certain cost structure is more profitable for the client based on predicted sales or usage.
- **Return on Investment (ROI)**: Demonstrate how your product could pay for itself over time.
- **Benchmark Data**: Compare your performance to industry averages or competitor stats, highlighting your advantages.

When you base your offers on credible data, the other side sees you as professional and well-informed, making them less likely to dispute your claims without evidence of their own.

13.18 Strategies for Small Businesses

Small business owners might face extra hurdles: limited brand recognition or budget constraints. They may be negotiating with bigger clients or suppliers who have more leverage. Some tips:

1. **Highlight Personal Service**: Large corporations can be slow or impersonal. Emphasize your speed, flexibility, and personalized approach.
2. **Show Growth Potential**: Even if you are small, prove your market is expanding. This can reassure bigger partners that you will be around long term.
3. **Lean on Local Networks**: Small businesses often form strong local ties. You might share references or success stories from nearby clients.
4. **Careful Cost Analysis**: Avoid underpricing to secure a deal. Ensure that the terms still allow you to stay profitable.

While it might feel intimidating, small businesses can succeed by pinpointing what they offer that others do not. Building a niche reputation can give you an edge.

13.19 Real-World Example: Supplier Contract

Imagine a medium-sized electronics firm that needs a steady supply of circuit boards. It negotiates with a supplier whose quality is high, but prices are above average. The electronics firm:

- **Researches** the supplier's raw material costs and labor rates, discovering that their standards require extra tests.
- **Proposes** a multi-year contract guaranteeing a set volume, in exchange for a price reduction.
- **Requests** a faster delivery schedule, offering a small premium for each batch delivered ahead of time to meet their own production deadlines.
- **Confirms** a clause specifying that if the supplier fails to meet quality checks three times in a quarter, the electronics firm can cancel the contract without penalty.

In this setup, the supplier enjoys a long-term client, while the electronics firm secures quality parts at a fair price. Both sides gain stability, which is often a major goal in business.

13.20 Golden Gem and Final Thoughts on Business Negotiations

Business negotiations require a blend of data-driven methods and relationship-building. Facts, figures, and clear contracts form the backbone of well-structured agreements. Meanwhile, human elements like trust, communication style, and cultural understanding can help close deals that last. Whether discussing salaries, forming joint ventures, or selling products, approach each interaction with respect and thorough preparation.

Golden gem: When the stakes are high, break down the negotiation into smaller parts. Solve easier points first to build momentum, and then tackle the tougher parts. This tactic can keep the conversation constructive and reduce the chance of a deadlock.

Next, we will explore negotiations in personal life (Chapter 14). While business deals often involve official contracts and profit targets, personal negotiations can also influence your day-to-day well-being, from household chores to major purchases like a car or home.

Chapter 14: Negotiations in Personal Life

Negotiation is not limited to the office or large transactions. Everyday situations—such as handling household budgets, sharing chores, or planning vacation spots—also involve discussions about who does what, when, and how. Personal negotiations may not always involve formal contracts or big sums of money, but they can still impact stress levels and relationships. This chapter shows how basic negotiation methods apply in friendships, families, and personal finances.

We will look at techniques for achieving agreements among family members, dealing with friends' requests without damaging the bond, and approaching significant personal purchases (like cars or houses) with a clear strategy. By learning to communicate calmly and find fair solutions in these small but important moments, you can reduce tension and maintain happier personal relationships.

14.1 Recognizing the Value of Everyday Negotiations

People sometimes think of negotiation as an activity for lawyers or salespeople. However, personal life is full of moments where two or more individuals want different things and must reach a common plan. Examples:

1. **Who Pays the Restaurant Bill**: Friends might each argue over paying or splitting equally.
2. **Roommate Chore Chart**: Deciding who takes out the trash or cleans the kitchen.
3. **Children's Bedtimes**: Children try to stay up later, parents want them to sleep on time.
4. **Vacation Plans**: One partner wants a beach trip, the other wants a mountain retreat.

Recognizing these small negotiations can help you prepare better, speak openly about your needs, and avoid letting minor differences lead to arguments.

14.2 Household Budget and Expenses

One of the most common personal negotiations involves money management in a household:

- **Bills and Shared Costs**: Partners or roommates might split rent, utilities, or groceries. How do you decide the share if incomes differ?
- **Spending Priorities**: Should surplus money go toward savings, a home renovation, or a nice dinner out?
- **Debt Repayment**: If one partner has debts, do both contribute to paying them off?

Key tips for budget talks:

- **Transparency**: Share accurate numbers about income and expenses.
- **Set Common Goals**: Agree on what you want to achieve financially—paying down debt, saving for a home, or setting aside an emergency fund.
- **Create a Simple System**: Use a joint account for shared bills or keep track using an app that monitors each person's contributions.
- **Revisit Often**: As incomes change or bills increase, re-evaluate how you split costs.

Approaching money talk calmly and logically reduces the chance of resentment. If you or your partner avoids the topic, small misunderstandings can become bigger problems later.

14.3 Sharing Chores and Responsibilities

Whether living with family, friends, or a partner, handling chores is a frequent source of tension. Nobody enjoys feeling they do more housework than others. A fair division requires:

1. **Listing Tasks**: Identify all chores (cleaning, cooking, shopping, laundry, pet care).

2. **Considering Preferences**: Maybe one person hates vacuuming but does not mind washing dishes. Another might enjoy cooking but hates grocery shopping.
3. **Agreeing on Frequency**: How often should floors be mopped or the trash taken out?
4. **Rotating or Swapping**: Some chores can be done in turns, preventing one person from always doing the same disliked task.
5. **Reviewing**: Every few weeks, check if the arrangement still feels balanced.

Sometimes it helps to post a schedule on the fridge or use a digital calendar. That way, each person sees their responsibilities clearly, reducing excuses or confusion.

14.4 Negotiating with Children

Parents often negotiate with kids about allowances, screen time, or bedtime. While children may lack an adult's logic, they still respond to fair discussions. Tips:

- **Set Clear Rules**: If a child wants extra TV time, tie it to finishing homework or doing a small chore.
- **Offer Choices**: Rather than a simple "No," give options. For instance, "You can watch 30 minutes of TV now, or 45 minutes later after your homework."
- **Explain Why**: Kids may follow rules more willingly if they understand the reason. "Sleep is important for your health" or "You need quiet time to focus on homework."
- **Stay Consistent**: If you give in every time a child whines, they learn to push harder. But if you hold firm on your agreements, they know the boundaries.

Parental negotiations aim to guide children toward responsibility while also respecting some of their preferences. Finding that balance can reduce daily conflicts at home.

14.5 Personal Friendships and Social Circles

Friends often request help, time, or resources. Negotiating politely is key to maintaining friendships:

- **Borrowing Items**: If a friend wants to borrow your car or equipment, clarify the return date or any usage rules.
- **Scheduling Outings**: Deciding on a date or activity can lead to disagreements about timing or cost. Suggest a few options and see if everyone can meet in the middle.
- **Attending Events**: Some friends might want you to attend gatherings that you do not enjoy. Propose a compromise: "I can join for the main part, but I'd like to leave after a couple of hours."

Friendship negotiations are often softer and less formal. Yet, respecting each other's boundaries and preferences keeps the bond strong. If you feel pressured, explain your limits honestly but kindly. Most friends will understand if you communicate clearly.

14.6 Buying or Renting a Home

One of the biggest personal negotiations is the purchase or rental of a home. This can be stressful because it involves large sums of money and personal preferences:

1. **Setting a Budget**: Know your maximum limit. Do not let a real estate agent push you above what you can realistically afford.
2. **Researching Market Conditions**: In a seller's market, you might compete with others, while in a buyer's market, you have more leverage.
3. **Property Inspections**: Request repairs or a lower price if the inspection reveals issues.
4. **Negotiating Rental Terms**: If you are renting, see if the landlord can include utilities in the rent or improve certain amenities for a slightly higher monthly fee.

5. **Handling Emotions**: People often feel emotional about a home, but keep your logic intact. If you overpay or accept bad terms, you might regret it.

In these high-stakes talks, small changes in price or interest rate can have a big impact on monthly payments. Prepare thoroughly and do not be afraid to walk away from a bad deal.

14.7 Car Purchases and Repairs

Another common personal negotiation is buying a vehicle or discussing repairs at an auto shop:

- **Car Price and Extras**: Dealerships might offer extras like extended warranties or paint protection. Decide in advance if those are worth the cost.
- **Trade-In Value**: If you have a car to trade, research its market value. Dealers often start with a low estimate, expecting you to push for more.
- **Financing Terms**: Look at the annual percentage rate (APR). A small percentage difference can change the total amount you pay over time.
- **Repair Costs**: If a mechanic gives a high quote, consider a second opinion. Ask for an itemized list of repairs so you understand what you are paying for.

Staying calm and using solid research prevents you from accepting overpriced deals or unneeded services.

14.8 Event Planning with Family and Friends

Organizing weddings, birthday parties, or family reunions often involves multiple people with different preferences. Conflicts might arise over the budget, guest list, or venue choice. Strategies include:

1. **Set Clear Roles**: Who is responsible for booking the location, managing invitations, or ordering food?
2. **Agree on Budget Upfront**: If parents or siblings are chipping in, clarify their contributions.
3. **Rank Priorities**: Is it more important to have a large gathering or a specific type of food? Focus on top priorities first, then fill in the rest.
4. **Compromise on Details**: If a family member insists on inviting many guests, ask them to cover any extra costs.

Such negotiations can be emotional due to family ties or personal traditions. A calm, step-by-step approach can keep things organized and reduce frustration.

14.9 Health and Lifestyle Choices

Loved ones might negotiate about diet, exercise routines, or lifestyle decisions. For instance, a couple might discuss whether to start a new fitness plan together. Or one partner might wish to adopt a certain eating style. Key points:

- **Respect Autonomy**: Do not force someone into a drastic lifestyle change if they are not ready.
- **Suggest Small Steps**: A huge change can be intimidating, but small steps feel more achievable.
- **Offer Mutual Support**: If you want your partner to join a gym, consider offering to go together.
- **Agree on Limits**: If one person wants to cut down on certain foods, clarify if the other can still have them in the house.

These talks require sensitivity because health is personal. Show genuine concern without pressuring. Negotiate ways to accommodate each other's choices in daily life.

14.10 Managing Extended Family Expectations

In some cultures, extended family members have significant influence on personal decisions—where to live, how to raise children, or even career moves. Negotiating with in-laws or other relatives can be delicate:

- **Clarify Boundaries**: Politely let them know which matters you consider private and which you welcome advice on.
- **Acknowledge Their Good Intentions**: They likely mean well, so thank them for caring, but explain your own perspectives calmly.
- **Set a Firm yet Polite Tone**: If an uncle constantly pushes a viewpoint, gently say, "We appreciate your thoughts, but we have decided to handle it this way for now."
- **Find Middle Ground**: If they request frequent visits or phone calls, see if you can schedule them in a way that fits your routine.

Balancing respect for family traditions with your own independence can reduce stress. Avoid letting these discussions turn into arguments by maintaining a polite approach.

14.11 Relationship Conflicts

Couples can face disagreements over communication styles, how to raise kids, or how to spend weekends. A constructive negotiation can help both parties feel heard:

1. **Listen Actively**: Let each person explain their viewpoint without interruption.
2. **Validate Feelings**: Acknowledge that their concerns make sense from their perspective.
3. **Seek Shared Solutions**: For instance, if one partner wants more social outings but the other prefers quiet weekends, agree to alternate: one weekend for social events, one for low-key activities.
4. **Stay Future-Focused**: Instead of blaming each other for past issues, discuss how to improve going forward.

Personal relationships thrive on mutual respect. If you approach problems as a team, looking for outcomes that meet both needs, you avoid winners and losers and encourage a more harmonious home.

14.12 Handling Peer Pressure

Adults face peer pressure, too, whether it is about social commitments or lifestyle trends. Negotiating your comfort level with peers might be subtle, but it is still relevant:

- **Know Your Limits**: If friends keep inviting you for expensive outings you cannot afford, politely explain your situation. Suggest cheaper alternatives.
- **Offer Compromise**: If a group often stays out late but you have an early job, agree to join for a few hours rather than the entire night.
- **Assert Boundaries**: If they push beyond what you can handle, politely but firmly say you are not able to do that.
- **Show Respect**: Avoid making them feel judged for their choices, just clarify you have a different approach.

Being open about your reasons can help friends understand. Peer pressure often eases if you communicate your boundaries confidently but kindly.

14.13 Negotiation with Service Providers

On a personal level, you might hire or negotiate with tutors, handymen, or private instructors. Consider these steps:

- **Set Clear Tasks**: Spell out the scope of work or lesson plan.
- **Discuss Rates Upfront**: Ensure you know if they charge hourly or per project.
- **Check References**: If possible, see how others rate them. This can guide whether their quoted fee is fair.
- **Agree on Milestones**: If the job is lengthy, set checkpoints to review progress and payment phases.

By treating service providers respectfully and clarifying expectations, you reduce the risk of disputes and often foster a better working relationship.

14.14 Confronting Awkward Situations

Sometimes personal talks touch on sensitive topics: a friend who owes you money but has not repaid, or a neighbor whose tree branches fall into your yard. It is tempting to avoid such issues, but addressing them can restore peace of mind:

1. **Stay Polite but Direct**: For instance, if your neighbor's tree is causing damage, say, "I noticed the branches are falling on my side, can we find a solution?"
2. **Propose Options**: "Would you be open to trimming the branches, or would you prefer I handle it if we split the cost?"
3. **Listen**: They might explain their financial constraints or fear of damaging the tree.
4. **Seek a Fair Outcome**: If there is a shared risk or cost, dividing responsibilities might be best.

Approaching these topics calmly, without blame, can often result in a compromise. Let them know you want to maintain a good relationship while resolving the issue.

14.15 Emotional Boundaries and Personal Well-Being

In close relationships, negotiations are not just about chores or money. They can also be about space, time alone, or emotional support:

- **Time for Hobbies**: A partner might want a few hours a week for a personal hobby. Negotiate schedules so neither feels neglected.
- **Emotional Support**: If a friend regularly vents about problems, decide how much time and energy you can offer without draining yourself.

- **Saying "No"**: It is okay to refuse requests that overwhelm you. You can say, "I would like to help, but I need some personal rest right now."

Protecting your well-being helps you be more present and supportive when you do engage. Setting these boundaries can be a form of personal negotiation that keeps relationships healthier over time.

14.16 Learning to Compromise in Daily Life

Compromise in personal settings does not mean one person always yields. It is about finding a balance:

- **Trade-Off**: If your roommate cooks dinner, you might clean the kitchen after.
- **Everyday Example**: If you want to go out for Italian food but your friend wants sushi, maybe alternate cuisines each week.
- **Fair Timing**: If you agree to a family gathering you are not thrilled about, you might request some alone time afterward to recharge.
- **Listening to "Why"**: Understand the reasons behind a request. If you discover your partner wants a quiet evening because they had a tough workday, you might be more open to adjusting your plan.

Small, day-to-day compromises can prevent resentment from building up. They also teach you to see the other person's perspective more frequently.

14.17 Conflict Resolution in Personal Life

When personal conflicts escalate, it might help to:

1. **Hold a Calm Conversation**: Pick a good time when neither side is rushed or stressed.
2. **Use "I" Statements**: Say, "I feel upset when…" rather than, "You always do this…"
3. **Seek Outside Help**: A counselor or neutral friend can moderate if the issue is serious.

4. **Look for Shared Interests**: Often both sides want peace and happiness, even if they disagree on how to get there.
5. **Aim for Understanding**: Instead of just winning, focus on learning what the other person truly cares about.

Personal conflicts can be as intense as business disputes. A structured approach helps ensure you find real solutions rather than blame each other.

14.18 Golden Rule: Respect and Communication

In personal negotiations, the "golden rule" of respecting the other person's dignity applies strongly. Whether it is dividing chores or deciding finances, humiliating or belittling someone can harm the relationship. Keep these points in mind:

- **Focus on the Issue, Not the Person**: Attack the problem, not their character.
- **Encourage Two-Way Input**: Let them suggest ideas rather than presenting your plan as the only option.
- **Stay on Topic**: Resist the urge to bring up unrelated past mistakes or unresolved arguments.
- **Apologize if Needed**: If you realize you were unfair or insensitive, a sincere apology can heal tension.

Respecting the other person fosters goodwill, making them more open to considering your viewpoint.

14.19 Real-World Example: Planning a Joint Vacation

A married couple wants a vacation. Person A loves the outdoors and Person B enjoys museums and city tours. They might:

1. **Discuss Budgets**: Agree on a total amount they can spend.
2. **List Possible Destinations**: Person A might name some national parks, Person B suggests popular cultural cities.

3. **Combine Activities**: Find a city near scenic trails or a region with both outdoor parks and local museums.
4. **Allocate Time**: Decide to spend the first half of the trip hiking and the second half exploring museums.
5. **Review Logistics**: Confirm transport, lodging, and daily schedules so both sides feel satisfied.

In this scenario, each partner's core interest is addressed. Neither feels forced to drop their preference entirely, and they craft an itinerary that integrates both sets of ideas.

14.20 Golden Gem and Conclusion

Negotiations in personal life can be just as influential as business deals. Agreements about chores, budgets, or social activities may not involve contracts, but they shape daily happiness and personal harmony. By using clear communication, active listening, and fair compromises, you can avoid misunderstandings that strain relationships.

Golden gem: Offer genuine understanding before insisting on your own point. A simple statement like, "I see why this matters to you," can reduce tension and invite them to be more flexible toward your wishes as well.

With this chapter, we see how negotiation tactics support respectful and balanced outcomes at home, with friends, and in personal finances. In the next sections, we will look at handling difficult negotiators (Chapter 15) and examine which tactics to avoid in negotiation (Chapter 16). These discussions will show how to protect yourself from manipulative or aggressive methods and remain ethical and calm under pressure.

Chapter 15: Handling Difficult Negotiators

It would be nice if everyone bargained in a calm, fair way. Unfortunately, some people use intimidating or misleading tactics to get what they want. In this chapter, we will explore how to deal with negotiators who are aggressive, manipulative, or uncooperative. These difficult styles can trigger strong emotions or confusion, which might lead you to accept bad terms. However, by learning to recognize key behaviors and using steady, logical responses, you can protect your interests while keeping the door open to a workable deal.

We will look at common difficult personalities, such as bullies, know-it-alls, silent stonewallers, and sneaky tricksters. We will discuss ways to stay calm under pressure, set boundaries, and turn a hostile atmosphere into one where fair solutions are still possible. We will also examine how to decide when it is best to end talks and walk away rather than tolerate ongoing bad behavior. By the end, you will have a set of tools to face challenging negotiators with more control and clarity.

15.1 Why Some Negotiators Behave Badly

Not every difficult negotiator is intentionally malicious. Sometimes, stress, fear, or lack of skill can cause negative behavior. For example, a person might feel overwhelmed by financial pressure and lash out to mask their anxiety. Others may copy tactics they saw in movies or read in books, wrongly believing that harshness is the only way to "win."

Still, some folks do use aggressive or manipulative methods on purpose. They see negotiation as a battle and want to "defeat" you. Recognizing the possible reasons behind their style can help you respond with less anger or shock. You can remind yourself that their rudeness often comes from insecurity or a flawed belief that intimidation works better than reasonable dialogue.

15.2 Identifying Common Difficult Styles

Though every negotiator is unique, certain negative approaches appear repeatedly:

1. **The Bully**
   - **Traits**: Loud voice, aggressive body language, threats, or insulting remarks.
   - **Goal**: Overwhelm you so you give in.
   - **Key to Handle**: Stay calm, speak in a measured tone, and do not mirror their hostility. Show that threats do not scare you into blind concessions.
2. **The Know-It-All**
   - **Traits**: Constantly lectures, claims superior knowledge, dismisses your ideas.
   - **Goal**: Make you doubt your own information and accept their terms without question.
   - **Key to Handle**: Politely ask for data to back their statements. Provide your own facts. Keep returning to objective sources rather than opinion.
3. **The Stonewaller**
   - **Traits**: Offers vague or minimal replies, refuses to engage, may sit silently in a meeting without contributing.
   - **Goal**: Make you propose all the ideas, hoping you will eventually drop your demands just to get a reaction.
   - **Key to Handle**: Ask direct questions. Be patient with silence, but clarify that progress requires two-way input.
4. **The Interrupter**
   - **Traits**: Cuts you off mid-sentence, never lets you finish, hijacks the conversation.
   - **Goal**: Prevent you from presenting your case fully, keeping control of the discussion.
   - **Key to Handle**: Calmly insist on completing your point. Sometimes you can say, "I'd like to finish my thought, and then I'm happy to hear your response."
5. **The Sneaky Tactician**
   - **Traits**: May tell half-truths, hide crucial information, or use small tricks like last-minute changes.

- **Goal**: Gain an unfair advantage by misleading or surprising you.
- **Key to Handle**: Request written confirmations, verify details with independent sources, and do not rush into signing anything you have not fully reviewed.

Real negotiators may combine these styles or switch between them. By naming the behavior, you reduce confusion and can choose a strategy to address it rather than feeling stuck.

15.3 Staying Calm and Grounded

Difficult negotiators often try to provoke an emotional reaction. If you get flustered or furious, you might say things you regret or forget your plan. Some methods to keep your cool:

- **Deep Breathing**: When you feel your heart racing, take a slow, deep breath in through your nose, pause, then exhale slowly through your mouth.
- **Pause Before Responding**: A brief silence can prevent impulsive outbursts. It also signals you are thinking, which can unsettle a bully expecting immediate compliance.
- **Focus on Facts**: Remind yourself of your main goals, your fallback plan, and the data you prepared. Stick to logic rather than matching their aggression.
- **Ask for Breaks**: If the tension is skyrocketing, suggest a short recess. Drink water, clear your head, and return with renewed focus.

By regulating your emotions, you deny them the satisfaction of controlling the mood. You stay in a better frame of mind to make rational decisions.

15.4 Setting Boundaries Firmly

One mistake people make is allowing rude or abusive behavior to continue. If you do not address it, the difficult negotiator assumes they can keep pushing. Instead, calmly but clearly state your boundaries:

- **Naming the Behavior**: For example, "I'd appreciate it if we could keep our tone respectful. We both want a workable agreement."
- **Requesting a Reset**: Suggest starting fresh after a break or calmly pointing out that insults are not productive.
- **Stating Consequences**: If they keep ignoring basic courtesy, you might say, "If we cannot continue respectfully, I'll have to end this meeting and revisit later."

This approach does not involve shouting or threats. It is about letting them know you notice the negative behavior, you do not accept it, and there is a clear outcome if it does not stop. Many bullies back off when they see you will not be intimidated.

15.5 Using Questions to Defuse Aggression

Asking calm, focused questions can steer a hostile negotiator away from personal attacks toward problem-solving:

1. **Clarifying Questions**: "Could you help me understand why that deadline is so strict?"
2. **Fact-Based Questions**: "How did you arrive at that price estimate? Do you have a source or data for it?"
3. **Solution-Oriented Questions**: "Is there a scenario in which you would accept partial payment now and the rest next month?"
4. **Reflective Questions**: "When you say this arrangement is unacceptable, what exact part concerns you most?"

Questions force them to explain. If they are bluffing or just throwing tantrums, they might struggle to answer logically. This can shift the conversation back to real issues instead of name-calling or intimidation.

15.6 Handling Threats and Ultimatums

"Take it or leave it." "If you do not agree now, the deal is off." These strong-arm tactics are meant to scare you. Rather than caving in:

- **Stay Curious**: Respond with, "Why is that your final position?" or "What leads you to such a strict cutoff?"
- **Check Their Bluff**: If you suspect they are bluffing, you can show you are willing to walk away unless they become reasonable.
- **Outline Your Conditions**: If you can only accept on certain terms, calmly say, "We can do that if you agree to a slightly longer timeline," or "We are prepared to end discussions if these terms are non-negotiable."
- **Do Not Rush**: Ultimatums often rely on pressure and haste. Slow down, examine your backup plan, and see if the threat is genuine or just a ploy.

Sometimes, an ultimatum might be real, but if the price or conditions are simply impossible, giving in may trap you in a bad deal. It might be better to stand firm or walk away.

15.7 Responding to Personal Insults

Nothing derails calm negotiation faster than personal attacks. If they mock your intelligence, experience, or background, do not retaliate with similar jabs. Instead:

- **Acknowledge the Insult Calmly**: "I hear your comment, but let's refocus on the contract terms."
- **Redirect**: "If you have concerns about my expertise, I can provide references or data. Otherwise, let's keep to the main points."
- **Set Boundaries**: "I ask that we keep this about the issue rather than personal remarks. Otherwise, I will end this session."

Refusing to engage on a personal level can stop the insult tactic from succeeding. Bullies thrive when they get an emotional rise out of you. By staying cool, you disarm them.

15.8 The Power of Silence

Many aggressive negotiators fill every silence with demands or arguments. You can use quiet pauses strategically:

1. **Let Their Words Sink In**: If they make an outrageous request, wait a moment without speaking. The awkward silence often prompts them to revise or clarify.
2. **Prevent Interruptions**: When you finish a statement, pause instead of rushing to fill space. This signals you are not afraid of quiet, giving them a chance to respond carefully.
3. **Show You Are Thinking**: Silence can convey that you are evaluating their points, not dismissing them with a quick comeback.
4. **Encourage Them to Talk More**: If they are trying to hide details, silence can prompt them to reveal more or fill in the gap.

Staying silent for a short, controlled period can be more powerful than trying to out-shout an aggressive person.

15.9 Checking for Hidden Allies

Sometimes, you face a panel of people in a meeting—one of whom is extremely difficult while others seem more balanced. Look for signs that others in their group might not approve of the aggression. Eye contact or subtle nods can suggest they feel uneasy. You can use that:

- **Address the Group**: Redirect questions to the calmer individuals, like, "How do the rest of you see this issue?"
- **Encourage Their Input**: Ask if anyone else has a perspective on the budget or timeline.
- **Build a Bridge**: If you gain the support of the moderate voices, the difficult member might be outnumbered in their hostility.

This does not mean you gang up on the aggressive person, but you show that reason and collaboration have broader support.

15.10 Negotiating in Writing or Email

Difficult negotiators may do better or worse when communication is written instead of face-to-face. Email can remove tone of voice or body language that escalates tension, but it can also create misunderstandings. If dealing with a hostile person:

- **Keep Messages Clear and Brief**: Emotional rants are less likely if your email is structured and factual.
- **Document Everything**: Written exchanges provide a record, preventing them from backtracking on promises or claiming you agreed to something else.
- **Do Not Respond in Anger**: If you receive a rude email, wait before replying. Craft a calm response that sticks to the main facts.
- **Suggest a Call If Needed**: Some clarifications might be easier in a quick phone chat than an email chain.

Written communication can slow down a bully's rapid-fire approach and give you time to craft thoughtful answers.

15.11 When to Seek Mediation or a Third Party

If a negotiator continues with bullying or dirty tricks despite your attempts to manage it, bringing in a neutral mediator can help. This person, often skilled in conflict resolution, can:

- **Set Ground Rules**: They may insist on no interruptions or insults.
- **Reframe Issues**: A mediator might restate each side's position in simpler terms, reducing emotional language.
- **Suggest Compromises**: They do not force a solution but can propose middle-ground ideas both sides may not see.
- **Protect the Process**: If one side tries to dominate or mislead, the mediator can call it out.

Mediation works well when both parties still want a deal but cannot communicate effectively on their own. If the other side refuses mediation, you must decide whether continuing is worthwhile.

15.12 Protecting Yourself Legally

Some difficult negotiators cross ethical or legal lines. They might lie about critical facts, conceal major defects in a product, or threaten you with harm. In such cases:

- **Keep Detailed Records**: Log every interaction, note any suspicious or threatening statements.
- **Pause the Talks**: If you suspect fraud or if you feel unsafe, stop negotiating until you can consult an attorney or relevant authorities.
- **Insist on Written Agreements**: Do not rely on verbal deals with someone who has shown dishonesty.
- **Know Your Legal Rights**: Depending on your region, you may have consumer protections, contract laws, or harassment rules that defend you from certain behaviors.

Safety and integrity come first. A bad deal is never worth risking personal harm or legal trouble.

15.13 Walking Away: The Final Option

In some negotiations, no matter how well you manage the situation, the other side remains too hostile or unethical. Knowing your backup plan (your alternative if this deal fails) is crucial. If that option is better than continuing with a toxic negotiation, it might be best to leave. Walking away:

- **Shows Strength**: It tells them you refuse to be bullied into a bad agreement.
- **Protects Your Resources**: Time, money, and mental energy can be saved for more productive endeavors.

- **Preserves Self-Respect**: You did not compromise your morals or well-being for the sake of closing a deal.
- **Opens Doors Elsewhere**: You might find a more respectful partner or a better job offer.

Yes, you may lose the immediate opportunity, but some deals simply are not worth the cost of dealing with an impossible counterpart.

15.14 Staying Professional Under Fire

Even if the other party acts unprofessionally, maintain your own standards. Avoid yelling, name-calling, or sending aggressive emails. This helps you:

1. **Keep a Good Reputation**: Others may hear how you handled a tough situation with composure.
2. **Think Clearly**: Professional behavior and calm thinking go hand in hand.
3. **Set an Example**: If you are in a group, your colleagues might follow your calm lead instead of descending into chaos.
4. **Maintain Credibility**: If the dispute ever goes public or legal, your calm approach will likely reflect better on you.

Staying civil does not mean being weak. You can be assertive and firm without stooping to their level.

15.15 Techniques to Redirect Focus

When a difficult negotiator tries to derail the talk with insults or side issues, redirect the discussion to the real topic:

- **Use "Let's Refocus" Statements**: "I understand your concern, but can we return to the payment terms now?"
- **Summarize Points**: "So far, we have agreed on the timeline, but the cost is still an issue. Let's settle that."
- **Separate People from Problems**: "I respect your viewpoint. Let's keep our attention on solving the budget gap."

These methods remind everyone why you are there. Do not let them steer the conversation into endless arguments or personal drama.

15.16 Building Your Confidence

Facing a harsh negotiator can be intimidating. Prepare by:

1. **Role-Playing**: Practice with a colleague or friend who acts out an aggressive style.
2. **Reviewing Facts:** Know your data so well that false claims or random attacks do not shake you.
3. **Positive Self-Talk**: Tell yourself you have a right to stand up for your interests.
4. **Learning from Past Wins**: Recall times you handled challenging talks successfully.

Confidence does not mean showing off or being arrogant. It means trusting your abilities and information enough that you are not easily rattled by hostility.

15.17 Adjusting Communication Channels

If in-person meetings are too charged, propose a phone call or written exchange. If they bombard you with angry emails, maybe a short face-to-face chat with a neutral observer present would be more manageable. Matching the communication channel to the situation can reduce the other side's ability to dominate or confuse you.

15.18 The Role of Empathy (Used Wisely)

While a bully might not deserve your sympathy, showing some level of understanding can sometimes soften their stance. For instance, if you sense their aggression comes from fear of losing a job, you might say, "I see this project is extremely important to you. Let's see if we can find terms that ease your concerns while also meeting our needs." This approach can reduce their anxiety-driven hostility. However, do not let empathy blind you to potential deception. Keep your guard up but stay open to legitimate worries they might have.

15.19 Example Scenario of Handling a Difficult Negotiator

Imagine you are discussing a lease for a storefront with a landlord known for tough tactics. He storms in, raising his voice about how "plenty of people want this space," belittles your business's small size, and demands a high rent immediately. You handle it by:

1. **Listening Calmly**: You let him vent without interrupting, making notes of key points.
2. **Asking Clarifying Questions**: "You mentioned strong demand for this space. Can you share recent offers or data on that?"
3. **Countering with Facts**: You show average local rent prices from a real estate report, pointing out that his request is 20% above the norm.
4. **Maintaining Composure**: When he insults your brand, you firmly state, "We treat this location seriously, and we want a fair deal that benefits both sides. I'm open to discussing a slightly higher deposit if it addresses your concerns."
5. **Setting Boundaries**: If he persists in yelling, you say, "I'd like to continue, but only if we can do so in a professional manner. Otherwise, I may have to consider a different property."
6. **Proposing a Break**: After a heated moment, you suggest stepping outside for a few minutes. When you return, the mood has cooled slightly.
7. **Reaching a Compromise**: He lowers the monthly rent in exchange for a three-year lease with a penalty for early termination, which you can accept if it remains within your budget.

This scenario shows that a calm approach, factual data, and clear limits often tame an aggressive person enough to find a workable deal—or reveal it is not possible.

15.20 Golden Gem and Conclusion

Dealing with difficult negotiators can feel draining, but with the right strategies, you can stay composed, protect your interests, and possibly still reach an outcome both sides accept. The key is to avoid falling into their emotional traps. Keep focusing on facts, use questions to draw out real issues, and be ready to walk away if their behavior is beyond reason. Remember that your calm, firm approach often sets a tone that even a hostile party might eventually respect.

Golden gem: Do not match their hostility. Keep your own tone respectful and your words clear. Difficult negotiators often lose power once they see you will not be intimidated or rattled.

With these tools, you can face aggressive, manipulative, or uncooperative parties with more confidence. In the next chapter (Chapter 16), we will examine specific negotiation tactics to avoid. Some methods seem clever in the short run but damage trust and reputations in the long term. By knowing which tactics are harmful, you can steer clear of them yourself and recognize when others use them on you.

Chapter 16: Tactics to Avoid

Negotiation is a process built on trust, information exchange, and a desire to find a workable outcome. However, some people use questionable tactics that break trust or undermine the long-term relationship. While these methods might bring short-term gains, they often cause more harm in the future—ruined reputations, legal troubles, or burnt bridges. In this chapter, we will explore tactics that you should avoid. We will also discuss how to spot these tactics if others try to use them on you, and how to respond in a firm but ethical way.

We will look at dishonest tricks, false promises, playing games with data, stalling on purpose, and other manipulations. You will learn why these moves backfire over time and how to handle them without lowering yourself to the same level. By keeping your negotiation style clean and ethical, you build a stronger foundation for future agreements.

16.1 Why Some People Use Unethical Tactics

Unethical or deceptive tactics usually come from fear or greed. A negotiator might lie because they are scared of losing or want to secure a big win. Some may never have learned better methods and believe shady tricks are normal. Others assume the other side is doing it, so they must do it too. However, even if you get away with these tactics once, the risks are high:

- **Loss of Credibility**: Once a client or partner realizes you lied, they may never trust you again.
- **Legal Consequences**: Fraud or misrepresentation can bring lawsuits or penalties.
- **Damaged Morale**: Team members who see dishonest behavior might lose respect for leaders or feel pressured to act similarly.

Short-term gains do not outweigh the long-term costs of losing your good name. A single dishonest negotiation can haunt your career for years.

16.2 False Promises

One of the most common tactics is promising something you cannot or will not deliver. This might include:

- **Claiming You Have Other Offers**: You pretend multiple parties want to buy at a high price, pressuring the other side to hurry. In reality, there might be no competing bids.
- **Overstating Capabilities**: Telling a client you can meet a strict deadline even though you lack the staff or materials.
- **Vague Commitments**: Saying "Yes, we can handle that" when you know there is only a slim chance of success.

Why it seems tempting: You might think it gets you a better deal or more time.
Why it is harmful: When the truth emerges—no rival offers, missed deadlines, broken promises—your reputation sinks. The other side feels tricked and may cancel the agreement or refuse future business.

Better Alternative: Be honest about your abilities and the interest level from other parties. If you are unsure, say so. It builds trust and avoids major fallout later.

16.3 Hiding Critical Information

Another tactic is withholding details the other side has a clear right to know. For example:

- **Selling a Car with Mechanical Issues**: Failing to mention known engine problems or major repairs needed.
- **Omitting Legal Constraints**: Not disclosing that local regulations forbid a certain activity included in the deal.
- **Skipping Risk Factors**: Keeping silent about a serious risk that could affect the project's success or safety.

Why it seems tempting: You might fear they will back away or force you to lower the price.
Why it is harmful: If the hidden facts emerge, you can face legal claims of misrepresentation or breach of contract. Even if not illegal, it creates a sense of betrayal.

Better Alternative: Provide all relevant facts. If it weakens your position, look for ways to offset that honestly—perhaps by adjusting price or offering warranties. Hiding the truth is never a stable foundation.

16.4 Fabricating Data or Credentials

In some cases, negotiators lie outright about their track record, finances, or references. They might:

- **Inflate Sales Figures**: Claim their product sells millions of units when it does not.
- **Forge Endorsements**: Quote fake testimonials.
- **Exaggerate Degrees or Titles**: Present themselves as a licensed expert when they are not.

Why it seems tempting: They think it lends credibility or impresses the other side.
Why it is harmful: If the other party does any checking, they will discover the lie. Once exposed, your trustworthiness is gone. You might also break laws about false advertising or fraud.

Better Alternative: If you do not have strong data, highlight your genuine strengths (like customer service or future growth plans). Build real credentials rather than faking them.

16.5 Playing Good Cop/Bad Cop Poorly

The "Good Cop/Bad Cop" strategy is sometimes seen in police dramas. In negotiations, two people from the same side pretend to disagree, with one acting mean and the other appearing friendly. The friendly one pressures you to accept a deal quickly before the "bad cop" returns with harsher terms. However:

- **Why it fails**: Many people recognize this trick. It feels staged and insincere. If both individuals are from the same team, you can suspect they coordinate these roles.
- **Why it is harmful**: It can annoy the other side, who realize you are attempting to manipulate them. Trust erodes quickly.

Better Alternative: If you have multiple negotiators, each can maintain a calm, consistent style. If you do have internal differences, be transparent about them or work them out privately before presenting a unified offer.

16.6 Endless Stalling

Some negotiators stall by refusing to commit, canceling meetings at the last second, or constantly claiming they need "final approval" from someone else. This can be a tactic to wear you down until you make major concessions out of frustration:

- **Why it seems tempting**: They believe you will get desperate, especially if you have a pressing deadline.
- **Why it is harmful**: It wastes time and can backfire if the other side finds an alternative partner while waiting. It also destroys goodwill. Nobody likes feeling strung along.

Better Alternative: If you need more time, be honest about why—perhaps you are waiting on a report. Propose a realistic date to reconvene. Continual stalling signals bad faith and might prompt the other side to leave.

16.7 Inflating Minor Issues

Another underhanded tactic is to blow up small concerns to gain concessions. For example, you might exaggerate a product's tiny flaw, acting outraged to force a bigger discount. Or if you are an employee negotiating salary, you may overstate how "terrible" the office environment is to push for a bigger raise.

- **Why it might seem to work**: The other side might cave to avoid conflict, especially if they worry you will walk away.
- **Why it is harmful**: Once they realize the exaggeration, you lose credibility for future requests. They may also regret giving in and try to undo it later.

Better Alternative: If there is a real concern, address it proportionally. Do not turn a small scratch into a catastrophe.

16.8 Personal Attacks or Ridicule

Some believe that mocking or insulting the other side can shake their confidence. They might make belittling remarks like "You clearly do not understand this market" or "Your business is too small to matter." This is a direct attack on dignity:

- **Why people try it**: They hope the insulted party will become unsure and more pliable.
- **Why it is harmful**: Personal attacks can lead to anger, halting all progress. It is also unprofessional and can brand you as a bully.

Better Alternative: Show respect. Even if you think the other side is inexperienced, politely explain your concerns or present data that clarifies the situation.

16.9 Creating Fake Urgency

"We can only hold this price for the next hour" or "The last unit is about to sell if you do not act." This false time pressure is designed to rush your decision. While some deadlines are real (like a limited sale or a manufacturing cycle), many are made up:

- **Why it sometimes works**: People fear missing out on a good deal and might jump in too soon.
- **Why it is harmful**: If it is exposed as fake, the other side sees you as dishonest. Also, they might question if any of your future deadlines are genuine.

Better Alternative: If a deadline or limited supply is real, show proof or explain why. Otherwise, let them decide at a natural pace.

16.10 Deliberate Misrepresentation of Authority

Some negotiators claim they have full power to sign a contract, then later say, "Oh, my boss must approve this." They use this to revise terms, forcing you to concede more. It is a type of "bait and switch":

- **Why do it**: They think you will be invested in the deal and not back out easily.
- **Why it is harmful**: You waste time and energy finalizing details with someone who was never truly authorized. This can strain relationships and cause mistrust.

Better Alternative: From the start, clarify who must sign off. If you are not the final decision-maker, let the other side know your role and which parts you can confirm.

16.11 Misuse of Confidential Information

Sometimes, you learn private details about the other side—maybe you discovered their real budget limit or personal struggles. Using that knowledge unethically to corner them is risky. For instance, if you know they need quick cash for an emergency, pressing them for a dirt-cheap price is exploitative:

- **Why it is tempting**: You might secure a big advantage.
- **Why it is harmful**: This crosses moral lines, can destroy trust, and cause resentment once they realize they were taken advantage of.

Also, it can spark public backlash if they reveal how you exploited private info.

Better Alternative: Respect sensitive details and use them only to craft fair solutions, not to squeeze the other side unfairly.

16.12 Threats or Intimidation

"I will ruin your reputation" or "I will sue you into bankruptcy." These scare tactics aim to force compliance out of fear:

- **Why people try**: They hope you will fold rather than risk a damaging fight.
- **Why it is harmful**: It might break laws against extortion or harassment. Even if not illegal, it permanently ruins trust. Many will call your bluff or report such behavior.

Better Alternative: If you have real legal concerns, handle them properly. Explain the possible legal outcomes calmly, without making wild threats.

16.13 Refusing to Listen at All

In some cases, a negotiator might pretend to hold "listening sessions" but ignores everything you say. They keep repeating their stance, blocking actual discussion. This is a tactic of stonewalling:

- **Why do it**: They think wearing you down will lead you to accept their demands.
- **Why it fails**: True negotiation requires both sides to talk and adjust. If one side is not listening, no real deal can form. It wastes time.

Better Alternative: Even if you have a strong position, hear their concerns. Real listening can reveal creative solutions.

16.14 Spotting These Tactics Used Against You

Be alert for signs that the other side is using these shady methods:

1. **Extreme Pressure or Sudden Deadlines**: Ask for proof.
2. **Inconsistent Claims**: They say one thing, then contradict themselves.
3. **Evasiveness**: They dodge questions about real authority or facts.
4. **Too Good to Be True Promises**: If it sounds unrealistic, it probably is.
5. **Emotional Manipulation**: Guilt trips, name-calling, or threats.

Once you suspect a bad tactic, you can calmly call it out or check with a neutral source. Ask for written clarifications. If they keep evading, consider walking away.

16.15 How to Respond without Sinking to Their Level

When you discover unethical moves:

- **Stay Polite but Firm**: "I'm not comfortable with that approach. Let's rely on verified data instead."
- **Ask for Transparency**: "Could you show me where you got those numbers?" or "Let's confirm the timeline in writing."
- **Propose a Better Way**: "Instead of rushing me with a fake deadline, let's schedule a reasonable date for a final decision."
- **Consider an End**: If they persist, you might say, "I respect the need for a deal, but I cannot continue under these conditions."

Refusing to cheat does not mean allowing yourself to be cheated. You can maintain ethical standards and defend your position.

16.16 Possible Consequences of Using Harmful Tactics

If you use these unethical methods:

- **Damaged Reputation**: Word spreads quickly, especially in tight-knit industries or communities.
- **Broken Deals**: The other side may cancel once they sense a trap.
- **Legal or Financial Risks**: Misrepresentation can lead to lawsuits or demands for refunds.
- **Stress and Guilt**: Acting unethically can cause personal stress or morale issues within your own team.

In short, the short-lived benefit rarely justifies the longer-term fallout. Ethical methods might take more effort, but they create stable results and better relationships.

16.17 Building Trust through Transparency

Trust is a powerful negotiation advantage. While you do not have to reveal every strategic thought, share enough information to make it easier for the other side to believe you:

- **Honest Timelines**: If you need a decision soon, explain why.
- **Real Numbers**: Show them how you arrived at a price or a budget figure.
- **Open Acknowledgement of Problems**: "We do have some production delays, but here is our plan to fix them."
- **Collaborative Attitude**: Invite them to ask questions or suggest alternative viewpoints.

Over multiple deals, your reputation for straightforward dealing can attract better partners and reduce suspicion.

16.18 How Ethical Negotiations Can Still Achieve Good Results

Some people fear that if they do not bend the rules, they will lose. That is not true. Skilled negotiators can reach favorable outcomes without trickery by:

1. **Being Well-Prepared**: Strong research on market rates, competitor offerings, and cost structures.
2. **Listening to Needs**: Understand the other side's real priorities. Propose solutions that solve their problems and secure your gains.
3. **Offering Creative Trade-offs**: Combine terms in ways that add value for both sides.
4. **Staying Firm on Key Points**: You can be assertive without being dishonest.
5. **Building Long-Term Bonds**: People prefer to partner with those who treat them fairly.

Ethical negotiation is not about being overly nice or naive. It is about using honest methods and well-planned strategies for mutual benefit.

16.19 Example of Avoiding a Harmful Tactic

Suppose you are selling a used car. You discover a small mechanical issue with the transmission. You might think, "I can hide this. The buyer might never notice for a while." But you realize:

- If they discover the issue, they could accuse you of fraud or demand their money back.
- They might leave negative reviews, scaring off future buyers if you ever sell another vehicle.
- You would feel uneasy about your dishonesty.

Instead, you disclose the issue up front, possibly offering to reduce the price slightly or fix it before the sale. The buyer appreciates your honesty and might still proceed, trusting you more. If they walk away, at least your integrity remains intact, and you avoid bigger trouble.

16.20 Golden Gem and Conclusion

Negotiation tactics that rely on lies, extreme pressure, or manipulation might yield a quick win, but they almost always lead to larger losses in trust and reputation down the road. By steering clear of such tricks, you show your reliability and foster more constructive discussions. Even if others try these methods on you, staying calm, calling out inconsistencies, and having the courage to walk away when necessary can protect you from unfair deals.

Golden gem: Ethical negotiation is not weakness. It is a strong approach that builds credibility and often leads to better partnerships over time. A single shady trick can destroy trust permanently, while honest methods keep opportunities open.

Having covered which tactics to avoid, we can now look forward to Chapter 17, where we discuss ethical standards in negotiation. In that chapter, we will explore how to define and maintain a moral code for conducting talks and how ethics shape professional and personal outcomes in the long run.

Chapter 17: Ethical Standards in Negotiation

Ethics in negotiation involves doing what is right rather than what is merely profitable in the short term. While some people see negotiation as a battlefield, a purely "win at any cost" approach can create serious problems later. By following ethical standards, you build trust that can give you an edge in both professional and personal settings. This chapter explores why integrity matters, how to set your own moral limits, and the value of transparency, fairness, and respect. We will look at real situations and see how a strong ethical stance can protect your reputation and help you reach stable agreements.

We will also talk about common ethical dilemmas and how to respond when someone pressures you to act against your code. By the end, you will have concrete steps for staying on the right path even when the stakes are high.

17.1 Defining Ethical Conduct in Negotiation

Ethical conduct means behaving in an honest, responsible, and respectful way toward all parties. It does not mean giving up your goals or losing out on important terms. Instead, it means staying within a moral framework:

1. **Honesty**: Telling the truth as far as the other side has a fair right to know. You do not have to reveal every strategic detail, but you avoid telling lies or half-truths.
2. **Fairness**: Seeking results that do not rely on tricking or pressuring the other side unfairly.
3. **Respect**: Treating the other side as people with valid interests and dignity.
4. **Responsibility**: Taking accountability if you make a mistake or fail to keep a promise.

Some people argue that ethics are optional in high-stakes deals. However, a pattern of unethical actions can ruin trust, cause partners to back out, or lead to legal conflicts. In contrast, negotiators with a known reputation for fairness often find that more people want to do business with them.

17.2 Why Ethics Matter

1. Reputation and Trust
Negotiators often rely on their track records. If word spreads that you are dishonest, many future partners will approach you with caution or avoid you completely. On the other hand, if you show consistency and integrity, people are more willing to open up and share real information. This makes negotiation smoother and can lead to deals that might not be possible if you had a shady record.

2. Long-Term Success
In many fields, repeat business and relationships provide more profit than single transactions. Unethical behavior might work once, but it usually ends future possibilities. Ethical negotiators earn repeat clients, referrals, and alliances. Over time, this leads to more stable growth and fewer crises.

3. Personal Peace of Mind
Many negotiators find that acting against their moral sense creates stress. They might worry about being found out or feel guilty about hurting someone else's interests. Working within an ethical framework reduces these anxieties. You can focus on doing a good job rather than hiding questionable actions.

4. Legal Safeguards
Laws in many places penalize fraud, deception, and similar wrongdoing. By sticking to ethical standards, you lower the risk of lawsuits or regulatory fines. You also protect your business or personal finances from the cost of legal battles.

17.3 Setting Your Own Code of Ethics

Before entering a negotiation, it helps to clarify what lines you will never cross. This personal code can cover areas like:

1. **Honesty in Facts**: Vowing never to lie about key data such as pricing, product quality, or budget constraints.

2. **Transparency in Capabilities**: Not overstating what you or your organization can deliver.
3. **No Personal Attacks**: Refusing to bully, insult, or undermine the other side's dignity.
4. **No Illegal Acts**: Firmly ruling out bribery, document falsification, or other legal breaches.
5. **Respect for Confidentiality**: If you have been trusted with private details, you do not misuse them for personal gain.

Writing these points down can help you remain strong if someone else pressures you to bend the truth or hide important facts. When you have a clear moral standpoint, it is easier to say no to tactics that violate your boundaries.

17.4 Truthfulness vs. Full Disclosure

An ethical negotiator should be honest, but that does not mean you must reveal every piece of private strategy. For instance, you do not have to volunteer your absolute bottom-line price if the other side has not asked, and they do not have an automatic right to that figure. However, if they ask a direct question—like whether a product has a known defect—you should not lie or hide critical problems.

Balancing honesty and strategic confidentiality means providing truthful answers about facts that the other side needs for a fair decision. Meanwhile, you are still free to keep certain negotiation tactics or fallback plans private. This principle helps you avoid deception while still protecting your legitimate interests.

17.5 Handling Pressure to Act Unethically

Sometimes, colleagues, bosses, or clients might push you to use dishonest methods. They might say, "Everybody does it," or "We need to do whatever it takes to close this deal." Here are ways to resist:

1. **Explain the Risks**: Point out how unethical behavior can harm future business or invite legal trouble.
2. **Suggest an Ethical Alternative**: Show how honest data and respectful dialogue can be effective.
3. **Seek Allies**: If you suspect that a supervisor is pushing unethical steps, you might find support among other team members who also want to do the right thing.
4. **Stand Firm**: If you cannot persuade them, you might refuse to follow unethical orders. This could be hard, but protecting your integrity may be worth the conflict.

Most organizations do not want to face lawsuits or public scandals. If you frame your refusal as protecting the company from reputational harm, you may find that others back down from their unethical demands.

17.6 Cultural Differences and Ethics

As discussed in Chapter 12, different cultures have varying norms about directness or negotiation style. However, basic honesty and respect are widely valued. In some places, giving small gifts might be normal, while in other places it could be seen as bribery. Knowing the local laws and traditions helps you avoid ethical missteps.

But universal principles—like not lying about safety or falsifying official documents—apply almost everywhere. Even if local culture tolerates certain gray areas, you still have the right to maintain higher standards if that aligns with your moral code.

17.7 Rejecting Bribes or Questionable Payments

In some industries or countries, people might casually suggest "extra fees" or "gifts" to finalize a deal. This can be a tricky situation, especially if it is normalized in the region. Before you agree:

1. **Check Local Laws**: Many places have strict rules against corrupt payments, even if they are common.

2. **Company Policy**: If you work for a firm, they likely have guidelines on what is allowed. Exceeding small gift limits could cause big problems.
3. **Alternatives**: You might politely decline by saying your organization's code of conduct does not permit it. Offer a genuine gift of appreciation, but keep it modest and within legal guidelines.

Paying or receiving bribes might open short-term doors, but the long-term risks are massive, including legal charges and a badly damaged name.

17.8 Avoiding Coercive or Abusive Tactics

Ethical negotiation rules out tactics that harm others in an extreme manner, such as threats, blackmail, or exploitation of personal struggles. If you discover the other side is in dire financial need, an ethical path does not mean you cannot negotiate firmly, but it does mean not pushing them to accept an unjust outcome that preys on their desperation.

Likewise, using personal secrets as leverage is frowned upon. If someone confides a private hardship to you, exploiting that knowledge to force them into a bad deal crosses a moral line. Remember that real success should come from fair terms, not from taking advantage of someone's vulnerability.

17.9 Transparency in Mistakes

No matter how careful you are, mistakes happen. For example, you might promise a delivery date and later learn you cannot meet it. Ethical behavior requires promptly admitting the error and proposing a solution, such as a partial refund or revised timeline. Hiding the mistake or blaming others might buy time, but it often inflames the problem when the truth emerges.

Owning up to mistakes can actually strengthen trust if you also show how you plan to fix them. People appreciate honesty and might be more forgiving if you address the issue instead of covering it up.

17.10 The Role of Ethics in Relationship Building

Negotiations often involve repeat interactions, especially in business. If you treat someone ethically today, they may return to you for more deals or speak highly of you to others. This referral power can be priceless. By contrast, if you treat them unfairly, you might "win" one deal but lose five potential future agreements.

Ethical approaches also help build a sense of goodwill that can carry over into tough negotiations. When conflict arises—such as a contract dispute—people who know you as fair and honest are more likely to give you the benefit of the doubt and work toward a friendly resolution.

17.11 Balancing Ethics and Competitiveness

Some people think ethics slow them down or reduce their edge. In reality, you can still be competitive and assertive while staying truthful. For instance, you can set a high asking price based on market research without exaggerating or lying. You can firmly negotiate for a bigger share of resources but remain polite and clear about your reasons.

Ethics do not mean surrender. They mean competing in a way that respects the boundaries of honesty and decency. Often, this style wins respect from the other side and reduces the chance of them retaliating or feeling tricked later.

17.12 Ethical Dilemmas in Team Negotiations

When negotiating as a group, some team members may suggest borderline tactics if they think it will help the collective. They might argue, "This is not personal. It's just business." If you disagree, handle it by:

1. **Discussing the Boundaries**: Clarify early in planning what the team's ethics policy is.

2. **Explaining Risks**: Let them know that unethical moves can backfire on everyone.
3. **Offering a Better Method**: Show them how to use strong data or strategic concessions instead of deception.
4. **Being Willing to Walk Away**: If your team insists on crossing lines you cannot accept, you may need to remove yourself from the process to protect your moral standing.

A unified approach to ethics can strengthen the entire team's credibility. If each member acts consistently, the other side sees you as reliable rather than suspicious.

17.13 Industry Standards and Regulations

In many sectors—finance, real estate, healthcare—there are rules on how deals must be disclosed or how data must be handled. Violating these can lead to professional penalties, canceled licenses, or fines. Ethical negotiators study these regulations and make sure they comply at every step.

Examples include:

- **Financial Transparency**: Publicly traded companies must release accurate information to shareholders.
- **Fair Housing Laws**: Real estate agents cannot hide available properties due to discrimination.
- **Privacy Rules**: Healthcare or tech firms must protect personal data.

Staying ethical means knowing these standards and following them strictly, even if bending the rules might offer a short-term edge.

17.14 Whistleblowing and Reporting

If you discover unethical behavior within your organization, you might face a tough choice: keep quiet or blow the whistle. Whistleblowing can be risky, but if serious wrongdoing is happening (fraud, harmful deception, or illegal acts), speaking up might be your moral duty. Some steps:

- **Document What You See**: Collect evidence rather than relying on rumors.
- **Check Reporting Channels**: Many companies or industries have ethics hotlines or compliance officers.
- **Seek Confidential Advice**: Consult an attorney if needed.
- **Protect Yourself**: Some places have laws shielding whistleblowers from retaliation, but you still need to be cautious.

While not a direct negotiation act, whistleblowing can arise if your team or boss repeatedly demands unethical steps. Doing what is right can prevent even larger harm down the road.

17.15 Responding to Unethical Actions from Others

You might encounter a negotiator who lies about product details or tries to bribe you. Depending on the severity, you can:

1. **Call Them Out Politely**: "I'm uncomfortable with this approach. Let's keep things aboveboard."
2. **Request Evidence**: Force them to prove claims if you suspect deceit.
3. **Decline or Walk Away**: If their entire style relies on dishonest methods, you might end the talks.
4. **Report If Illegal**: In cases of fraud, bribery, or blackmail, consider alerting relevant authorities or professional bodies.

Do not tolerate ongoing dishonesty. Even if you want the deal, enabling unethical behavior invites more problems later. Setting firm boundaries may also push them to negotiate more honestly.

17.16 The Importance of Consistency

Ethics is not a one-time choice. You must consistently apply your standards. If you cheat in a small negotiation but act fair in a larger one, word of that inconsistency might leak out. People then wonder which version of you they are dealing with.

Consistency also means setting the same rules for yourself that you expect from others. If you demand transparency from the other party, you should practice it too. Fairness remains more convincing when you exemplify it in your own behavior.

17.17 Examples of Ethical Negotiation in Action

1. **Salary Talk**: You know the typical range for your position. You state your achievements clearly and ask for a fair raise. You do not lie about having other job offers if you do not.
2. **Supplier Contract**: You share accurate projections of your needed quantity, not faking higher numbers to push for a discount. If the supplier struggles with a short timeline, you discuss partial deliveries rather than threatening them with false penalties.
3. **Family Estate**: Relatives negotiate dividing inherited property. You reveal all known assets to your siblings, instead of hiding some. Everyone sees you as trustworthy, making the process smoother.

These are not "soft" approaches; they are strong, clear, and respectful. By upholding honesty, you reduce suspicion and speed up the process toward a balanced deal.

17.18 Teaching Ethical Values to Your Team

If you manage or mentor others, lead by example. Encourage open conversations about ethics. Provide scenarios and ask, "How would you handle this if a client wants us to falsify a document?" This training helps your group form a shared understanding of right and wrong in negotiations.

You can also recognize and praise team members who handle tough talks ethically. Positive feedback shows that your organization values integrity, not just results at any cost.

17.19 The Long-Term Payoff of Ethical Behavior

Ethics may sometimes cost you a quick win if you refuse to lie or hide a problem. But the benefits often appear in the form of stable partnerships, repeat business, and a respected brand. Over years, ethical negotiators build networks of people who trust them. That trust can open doors to bigger deals and faster agreements, since less time is wasted verifying every claim.

Moreover, an ethical stance means you can sleep better at night, knowing you did not take advantage of anyone or engage in questionable acts that could haunt you later.

17.20 Golden Gem and Conclusion

Sticking to ethical standards is not just about following rules—it is about protecting your credibility, nurturing stronger relationships, and avoiding the hidden traps that come with dishonest actions. While it might seem challenging in a world where some believe you must do anything to win, honesty and fairness remain the foundation for success that lasts.

Golden gem: Ethics in negotiation does not weaken you. It makes you a trusted, reliable partner whose word carries real weight, giving you an advantage that unethical players can never match in the long run.

With these principles in mind, you can maintain a high moral ground, build a good name, and still secure favorable outcomes. Next, we will look at technology and digital negotiation (Chapter 18), exploring how modern tools like video calls and online platforms affect communication, data sharing, and security in today's world.

Chapter 18: Technology and Digital Negotiation

Digital tools have transformed how we conduct negotiations. From emails and instant messages to video conferencing and specialized platforms, technology allows people to connect worldwide in seconds. Yet online communication changes the dynamics of negotiation, sometimes creating new challenges. In this chapter, we will look at the opportunities and pitfalls of digital negotiation, as well as best practices for using technology effectively and securely.

We will explore how to maintain clarity in written exchanges, the pros and cons of video calls, the rise of online marketplaces, and how to protect sensitive information in a digital age. By understanding these factors, you can adapt your negotiation style to modern settings without losing the personal touch that often makes deals successful.

18.1 How Technology Has Changed Negotiation

Not long ago, major negotiations required physical meetings or phone calls. Now, a deal can be finalized through chat messages, video conferencing, or specialized contract-signing apps. This shift brings several benefits:

1. **Speed and Convenience**: You can email a proposal instantly, reducing travel time and costs.
2. **Global Reach**: You can negotiate with people across continents without leaving your desk.
3. **Data Analysis**: Digital tools let you share spreadsheets, link to market data, and present live graphs.
4. **Easy Record-Keeping**: Email archives and file storage let you store proposals and finalize terms securely.

However, technology also introduces issues like misunderstandings due to lack of face-to-face cues, security risks (like hacking), and potential over-reliance on text instead of real conversation.

18.2 Email Negotiations: Pros and Cons

Advantages

- **Written Record**: Everything is documented, so you can review the exact wording later.
- **Time to Think**: You can craft careful responses rather than reacting under pressure.
- **Convenience**: You do not have to schedule a live meeting for each small point.

Disadvantages

- **Limited Tone and Context**: It is easy to misread the intended tone. A statement that seems neutral to you might offend the other side if read differently.
- **Delayed Responses**: If the other person is busy or in a different time zone, waiting for replies can slow progress.
- **Risk of Overuse**: Email chains can become very long, with repeated clarifications needed for complex topics.

A good practice is to keep emails clear and concise. Use bullet points or short paragraphs for key terms. If confusion arises, consider a quick call or video session to resolve it faster.

18.3 Video Conferencing: Advantages and Tips

Video conferencing platforms—like Zoom, Microsoft Teams, and others—allow you to see facial expressions and hear tone of voice. This provides more cues than text or phone calls. Some guidance for success:

1. **Check Your Tech**: Test your camera, microphone, and internet connection beforehand. Technical glitches can kill momentum.
2. **Professional Setting**: Choose a clean, quiet space. Dress in a way that matches the formality of the discussion.

3. **Watch Body Language**: Even over video, eye contact matters. Look into the camera sometimes instead of just at the screen.
4. **Manage Screen Sharing**: If you present slides or documents, rehearse how to switch screens smoothly.

Video calls can mimic face-to-face interactions, but be mindful of possible time delays or background distractions. Also, if participants speak different languages, consider turning on real-time captions or having a translator on standby.

18.4 Instant Messaging and Chat Apps

Some negotiations, especially smaller ones or quick clarifications, happen over chat services like Slack, WhatsApp, or similar platforms. These can be effective for:

- **Rapid Exchanges**: You can ask a question and get an immediate response if the other person is online.
- **Informal Communication**: Chat can feel more relaxed than email.
- **Group Collaboration**: Multiple people can join a group chat, sharing updates in real time.

Yet problems arise if critical decisions are made in a rush. Also, chat apps may mix personal and professional contexts, increasing the chance of sending a message to the wrong group or losing important details among casual talk. For significant changes, always document them in a more official format, like a follow-up email or a saved transcript.

18.5 Online Platforms for Negotiation and Auctions

Certain digital platforms specialize in buying, selling, or trading goods and services. Examples include eBay for consumer goods or specialized marketplaces for business supplies. Some key points:

1. **Set Clear Terms**: If you sell something on a marketplace, state your conditions (shipping, returns, payment) upfront.

2. **Bidding and Auctions**: Understand the rules for bidding. Some platforms have strict policies about retracting bids or dealing with non-paying buyers.
3. **Reputation Systems**: Many sites use seller or buyer ratings. Maintaining a good rating is vital for trust.
4. **Dispute Resolution**: Online platforms often offer built-in procedures if a buyer or seller claims a problem.

Digital marketplaces can connect you with more potential partners than ever, but also bring competition from other sellers worldwide. Maintaining honesty in listings and prompt communication helps you stand out in a crowded online space.

18.6 E-Signatures and Digital Contracts

Signatures no longer have to be on paper. Many legal systems accept electronic signatures as valid. Tools like DocuSign or Adobe Sign let you send a contract link; the other party can click through, sign digitally, and send it back. Benefits include:

- **Faster Turnaround**: No need to mail or fax documents.
- **Automatic Record**: The system records date, time, and user details.
- **Secure Storage**: Both sides can keep digital copies.

Watch for local laws: some countries have extra rules about e-signatures. Also, make sure the contract is clear and check that the other side is truly authorized to sign digitally.

18.7 Cybersecurity and Data Privacy

When negotiating online, you often share sensitive details: prices, proprietary data, or personal information. Hackers or unauthorized people could steal or intercept these if security is weak. Steps to stay safe:

1. **Use Encrypted Channels**: Email services or messaging apps that offer end-to-end encryption reduce the chance of snooping.

2. **Check URLs**: Be sure you are on the correct site (especially for e-signing) and watch for phishing attempts that mimic known services.
3. **Password Protection**: Use strong, unique passwords for negotiation portals or file-sharing platforms.
4. **Limit Access**: Only share negotiation files with people who need them. Revoke permissions once the process is over.

Data breaches can ruin trust. If the other side suspects you cannot guard their information, they might back out or push for extra legal measures. A strong security posture shows professionalism.

18.8 Recording Meetings and Consent

Some video tools let you record calls. While that can be useful for revisiting details, you should always get consent if you plan to record. In many places, recording someone without their knowledge or permission is illegal or unethical. Even if the law allows one-party consent, it can harm trust if they discover you recorded them secretly.

If you want a record of the talk, say so upfront and ask if it is okay. Alternatively, take written notes and confirm them in an email after the meeting. This transparency keeps you aligned with ethical standards and preserves trust.

18.9 Nonverbal and Emotional Cues Online

Face-to-face negotiation benefits from direct observation of posture, facial expressions, or tone. Digital negotiation reduces these signals. Even on video, you only see a limited view, and subtle movements might be lost. In text-based communication, you have zero visual clues. To compensate:

- **Use Clear Language**: In chat or email, use polite and precise words. Avoid sarcasm or jokes that might be misread.

- **Ask for Feedback**: "Does that make sense?" or "How do you feel about this proposal?" can open the door for the other side to express concerns.
- **Look at Response Times**: If someone takes a long time to reply, they may be uncertain or not fully on board. Check in politely.
- **Schedule Video Calls for Complex Issues**: If text alone might cause confusion, propose a quick video meeting.

Understanding emotional states online can be hard. Prompt, respectful communication helps reduce misunderstandings.

18.10 Time Zone and Scheduling Challenges

Global digital negotiation involves coordinating across different time zones. This can slow progress or require calls at odd hours. Tips:

1. **Plan Ahead**: Know each participant's local time. Suggest meeting windows that are fair for everyone.
2. **Rotate Inconvenient Times**: If you have recurring calls, alternate who must get up early or stay late.
3. **Use Shared Calendars**: Online calendars can show everyone's availability at a glance.
4. **Allow Async Updates**: If scheduling is too hard, handle many details by email or shared documents, then do occasional live calls for big decisions.

Being flexible and considerate of others' schedules builds goodwill. They appreciate you are not ignoring their constraints.

18.11 Building Trust Online

When you cannot shake hands in person, building trust digitally requires extra effort:

- **Professional Profiles**: If you are on LinkedIn or a company site, keep your information updated so people can verify your credentials.

- **Share References**: Provide links to testimonials, case studies, or industry articles featuring your work.
- **Keep Promises**: If you say you will send a file by 5 p.m., do it. Reliability is key, especially online where flakiness is common.
- **Prompt Responses**: Even a short "Received your message, will reply soon" can show you value their time.

Regular, clear, and polite communication can offset the lack of face-to-face contact. Over time, these habits prove you are dependable.

18.12 Handling Disputes in Digital Spaces

If disagreements arise, the same conflict-resolution principles apply, but the medium is different. Options include:

1. **Private Messaging**: Take the issue into a direct chat with the key person rather than a public forum.
2. **Group Calls**: If multiple parties are involved, a video or conference call might be best to clear the air.
3. **Mediation Tools**: Some platforms or third-party services provide online dispute resolution.
4. **Public Reviews**: On marketplaces, users can leave negative or positive feedback. Respond calmly if you face a complaint. Offer to fix the situation rather than arguing publicly.

Remaining calm and respectful, even when you feel wronged, preserves your reputation. Digital hostility can escalate fast, so it is wise to solve issues privately where possible.

18.13 Balancing Digital and In-Person Interaction

Sometimes, an entirely online negotiation is fine—especially if the stakes are lower or the transaction is straightforward. For more complex deals or sensitive topics, a mix of online and face-to-face might be ideal. You could:

- **Start with Video Calls** to introduce each side and share main goals.

- **Exchange Drafts by Email**, refining the contract details.
- **Meet in Person for Final Signing** or a key milestone if feasible.

Each channel has pros and cons. Combining them can help you maintain speed, clarity, and personal rapport.

18.14 Culture and Language Barriers Online

When you negotiate with people from different backgrounds, technology can either help or complicate cultural gaps. Automated translation tools can assist, but they are not always accurate. Some tips:

- **Use Simple Language**: Avoid jargon or slang that machine translators might mangle.
- **Check Meanings**: If the other party uses a phrase that seems unclear or odd, politely ask them to clarify.
- **Be Aware of Etiquette**: Some cultures find quick, direct messages abrupt, while others appreciate brevity.
- **Confirm Key Points**: Summarize agreements to ensure you both understood the same thing.

Patience and respect help prevent small misunderstandings from becoming major obstacles.

18.15 Automation and AI in Negotiation

Artificial Intelligence tools can analyze contracts, compare market rates, or even generate suggested responses. While these tools are growing, they are not a substitute for human judgment. They can help with:

- **Data Analysis**: Sorting through large sets of offers or typical market standards.
- **Drafting Basic Contracts**: Automated templates that fill in known details.
- **Predictive Outcomes**: Some advanced systems predict the likelihood of acceptance at certain price ranges.

However, AI may lack nuance in emotional or context-rich conversations. Rely on it for repetitive tasks but keep human insight at the center of your strategy. Always review AI-generated content for accuracy and tone.

18.16 Privacy Concerns and Third Parties

Online negotiations might involve third-party platforms. Check their privacy policies: do they store messages or share them with advertisers? If confidentiality is critical—like in mergers or sensitive personal matters—choose secure channels. You can also use Non-Disclosure Agreements (NDAs) that bind all participants, including platform operators if needed.

When dealing with large corporate deals, your IT department may set up a secure virtual data room. This is an online repository for documents, accessible only to authorized parties. Logging and tracking features help ensure no unauthorized viewing or leaks.

18.17 Avoiding Digital Rudeness

The ease of sending quick messages can lead to abrupt or harsh wording. In digital communication, the other side cannot hear your tone or see a friendly smile. They may interpret an innocent short message as cold or annoyed. To prevent this:

- **Use Polite Greetings**: Even brief chats can begin with "Hi [Name], hope you're doing well."
- **Short Apologies for Delays**: If you could not answer quickly, say, "Sorry for the late response."
- **Avoid Using ALL CAPS**: Some see it as shouting.
- **Double-Check for Sarcasm**: Jokes can fail if the recipient does not catch your humor. Use clarity or skip sarcasm in serious talks.

A small effort to be courteous can maintain a positive vibe, especially when you do not have in-person warmth to rely on.

18.18 Real-World Example: Remote Contract Negotiation

Imagine you own a small tech startup in Europe and want to partner with a distributor in Asia. You begin with an introductory email, showing product details and references. They respond positively, so you move to a video call. Over a few weeks, you exchange draft contracts via a secure e-sign platform. Each step:

1. **Email**: You clarify each contract clause in short messages, attach updated versions, and keep a clear subject line for easy reference.
2. **Video Meetings**: You schedule calls at a time that suits both time zones (morning for you, late afternoon for them). Everyone checks their connections, and you share slides showing market prospects.
3. **Digital Security**: You store all proposals in an encrypted folder, giving the other side controlled access.
4. **Cultural Awareness**: You notice they prefer more formal addresses. You keep your language polite and avoid slang.
5. **Final E-Sign**: Once final terms are settled, you use an e-sign tool. Both sides sign electronically and get PDF copies.

The entire deal happens without an in-person meeting. By consistently using respectful language, verifying details in writing, and addressing any confusion quickly, you reach an agreement that both sides trust. This scenario shows how technology can bridge distances and accelerate deals, provided you manage it carefully.

18.19 Future Trends in Digital Negotiation

We can expect further developments:

- **Virtual Reality Meetings**: Some companies experiment with VR rooms where avatars meet. This might give more immersive cues than basic video.

- **Smart Contracts**: With blockchain technology, contract terms can automatically execute when certain conditions are met (like releasing payment upon delivery confirmation).
- **AI-Driven Insights**: More advanced algorithms could analyze real-time data to suggest optimal deals or detect if the other side's demands are unrealistic based on market trends.
- **Voice-Enabled Tools**: Systems that transcribe and summarize calls in real time could cut down on note-taking errors.

Adapting to these innovations will be important, but the core negotiation skills—like empathy, clarity, and fairness—will remain central, no matter how advanced the tools become.

18.20 Golden Gem and Conclusion

Technology has opened new doors for negotiation, offering speed, global reach, and data-driven insights. Yet it also poses risks like misunderstandings, security breaches, and reduced personal rapport. The key is to combine the benefits of digital tools with the timeless human elements of respect, honesty, and clear communication. Keep security strong, manage your online tone, and switch to more personal channels—like video or phone—whenever you sense confusion or heightened sensitivity.

Golden gem: A well-balanced approach to digital negotiation uses technology for efficiency but preserves human warmth and clarity. Quick messages and e-signatures can speed deals, but do not let screens replace the genuine human connection that fosters mutual trust.

Next, we will look at continuous improvement in negotiation (Chapter 19). Negotiation is a skill that grows through practice, feedback, and reflection. By integrating lessons learned from both online and offline talks, you can refine your style and become more effective over time.

Chapter 19: Continuous Improvement

Negotiation is not a skill you learn once and then master forever. Conditions change, people's expectations shift, and your own goals evolve as you gain experience. Continuous improvement is the process of regularly examining your negotiation habits and outcomes, looking for ways to become more effective and flexible. Think of it as an ongoing process of refining your approach, building on successes, and learning from mistakes.

In this chapter, we will discuss practical steps for evaluating your negotiation performance, collecting feedback, and setting development targets. You will see how to track your progress, find areas that need attention, and gradually raise your proficiency. By making small but consistent efforts, you can keep your negotiation abilities sharp and relevant, no matter how the environment around you changes.

19.1 Why Continuous Improvement Matters

Some people think that once they have read a book or attended a workshop on negotiation, they are all set. But real growth comes from applying ideas, testing them in live situations, and analyzing what went right or wrong. Continuous improvement matters because:

1. **Changing Markets**: If you operate in business settings, market prices, consumer trends, and competitor behavior never stand still. What worked last year might not succeed now.
2. **Evolving Relationships**: Over time, you build new ties and face new personalities. Each new relationship can demand fresh communication methods.
3. **Personal Growth**: As you gain confidence, you can experiment with advanced techniques or bigger goals. But with each higher level, you face fresh challenges.
4. **Avoiding Complacency**: Without regular evaluation, you might rely on old habits that no longer fit your circumstances.

Much like an athlete who constantly trains to remain competitive, negotiators who embrace ongoing learning keep their edge. This leads to better outcomes, smoother talks, and more opportunities to find creative, fair solutions.

19.2 Key Areas for Self-Review

When you want to improve, you need a focus. It is easy to say, "I want to be a better negotiator," but that is too vague. Here are some concrete areas you can examine:

1. **Preparation Quality**: Did you research thoroughly, define clear goals, and plan your possible concessions?
2. **Communication Skills**: Did you express your points clearly? Did you listen actively, or did you talk over the other side?
3. **Emotional Control**: Were you calm under pressure, or did frustration lead you to make rash decisions?
4. **Adaptability**: Did you adjust to unexpected demands or cultural nuances, or did you stick rigidly to a script?
5. **Outcome Satisfaction**: Even if you "won" on price, was the other side's experience poor, risking future conflict?

Breaking negotiation into these categories lets you pinpoint strengths and weaknesses. For example, you might find you prepare well but struggle with staying calm during sudden surprises. That insight guides you on what to practice next.

19.3 Keeping a Negotiation Journal

A practical way to track growth is by maintaining a journal or a digital log. Each time you finish a negotiation—no matter how small—take a few minutes to record:

1. **Date and Context**: Who was it with, and what was the subject?
2. **Your Goals**: What did you aim to achieve, and did you have a fallback plan?

3. **Main Points Discussed**: Briefly summarize the crucial topics, offers, and counteroffers.
4. **Outcome**: Did you reach an agreement? Were you satisfied with it?
5. **Key Observations**: What techniques worked? Where did you stumble? Did you notice emotional triggers?

By reviewing these entries periodically, patterns emerge. You might see that certain types of negotiators frequently cause you stress, or that your best outcomes happen when you do specific research first. This is direct evidence that helps you adjust your methods.

19.4 Seeking Feedback from Others

Sometimes, we cannot see our own blind spots. Getting input from trusted colleagues, friends, or mentors can speed up improvement. If possible, invite a neutral observer to watch or listen (with permission) to a negotiation, or at least debrief with someone who was present. Ask them:

- **Which parts of my presentation were convincing?**
- **Did I interrupt or ignore any signals from the other side?**
- **Did I manage my tone and body language well, or did I appear impatient or aggressive?**
- **Where did I seem uncertain or underprepared?**

Even if you only get a few remarks, they can spotlight specific issues you may never notice on your own. If you have a mentor with deep negotiation experience, they may share suggestions for alternative tactics or angles you overlooked.

19.5 Monitoring Results Over Time

Improvement is easiest to track if you have some metrics. These can be qualitative or quantitative. For instance:

1. **Success Rate**: Out of all negotiations in a month, how many ended in a deal that met your core needs?

2. **Average Concession**: Do you consistently give up more than you planned, or have you learned to secure balanced trade-offs?
3. **Time to Agreement**: Are you reducing the back-and-forth cycles with clearer proposals?
4. **Relationship Quality**: How many repeat agreements or positive references do you get?

Compare these numbers every few months. If you see that your success rate jumped from 50% to 70%, or that you can close deals faster without sacrificing value, it indicates progress. If numbers dip, that might signal you need to revisit your approach.

19.6 Adapting to Changing Environments

Continuous improvement also involves staying up to date on new factors in your negotiation landscape. For business deals, this could mean:

- **Economic Shifts**: Inflation, currency fluctuations, or job market trends that affect wages or prices.
- **Regulatory Changes**: New laws or policies that alter contract terms, consumer rights, or industry rules.
- **Technological Advances**: Tools that influence how negotiations are done, such as data analytics or specialized platforms (as discussed in Chapter 18).

In personal negotiations, the landscape might be:

- **Evolving Family Dynamics**: New responsibilities or changes in household finances that require a fresh approach to budget or chores.
- **Social Shifts**: Changes in your circle's norms, like how friends split bills or plan joint activities.

By recognizing shifts early, you can update your negotiation strategies to match the new reality, rather than clinging to outdated methods.

19.7 Embracing New Techniques Carefully

Sometimes, you might be tempted to try an advanced negotiation trick you read about, like a certain anchoring move or a creative discount structure. While innovation is good, test new techniques in lower-stakes settings first. If you attempt something very risky during a high-stakes talk without practice, you could cause confusion or undermine trust.

Try the following steps:

1. **Research the Method**: Understand the logic behind it. Is it suitable for cooperative or competitive environments?
2. **Role-Play with a Friend**: Practice how it would sound if someone used it on you. Identify potential pitfalls.
3. **Apply in a Smaller Negotiation**: If possible, test it in a simpler context—like discussing chores or a minor purchase.
4. **Analyze Outcomes**: Did it produce a better result or cause complications?

Gradually adopting new techniques helps you refine them until they feel natural and ethical.

19.8 Overcoming Personal Plateaus

It is normal to reach a point where you do not feel any real growth. Maybe you keep repeating the same negotiation style, or you no longer see improvement in results. To get past this:

- **Try a Different Setting**: If you mostly negotiate internally at work, look for volunteer or community situations to apply your skills with new people.
- **Attend Advanced Workshops**: Seek courses or seminars that push you beyond your comfort zone.
- **Get a Mentor or Coach**: A seasoned negotiator can provide targeted insights.
- **Study Case Histories**: Reading about complex negotiations—business mergers, diplomatic treaties—can reveal strategies you have not considered.

Plateaus often occur when you are comfortable with a routine. Challenging yourself in fresh environments forces you to adapt and learn anew.

19.9 Creating a Personal Development Plan

Instead of random improvement, set specific goals with timelines. For instance:

1. **Short-Term Goal**: "Within three months, I want to reduce the average time I spend reaching a basic agreement by 20% by focusing on clearer opening offers."
2. **Medium-Term Goal**: "Within six months, I plan to raise my success rate in supplier negotiations from 60% to 75% by doing deeper market research and testing a new approach to concessions."
3. **Long-Term Goal**: "In one year, I aim to handle cross-cultural talks more confidently, finishing at least three deals with partners from different countries."

Document these aims. Then, track your progress. Check monthly or quarterly if you are moving in the right direction. Adjust your plan if conditions change or if you realize your targets were too easy or too difficult.

19.10 Formal Training and Education

Some negotiators benefit from structured courses, either online or in-person. These may include:

- **Workshops**: Focus on role-playing exercises, giving you real-time feedback.
- **University Programs**: Courses on conflict resolution or business negotiation, which can provide a deeper academic perspective.
- **Professional Certifications**: Certain industries offer credentials verifying advanced negotiation or conflict management skills.

Formal education can expose you to different theories (like distributive vs. integrative bargaining) and proven frameworks (like the Harvard Negotiation Project). Just be sure to apply what you learn in actual deals, or the knowledge remains abstract.

19.11 Learning from Failure

No matter how skilled you get, some negotiations will fall apart or produce less-than-ideal results. In these moments, it is easy to feel discouraged. But failure often reveals your greatest opportunities for growth. Ask yourself:

- Did I Misread the Other Side's Needs?
- Were My Goals Unrealistic from the Start?
- Did I Lose Emotional Control or Rush a Decision?
- Was There a Way to Offer More Value Without Huge Concessions?

Failure becomes valuable if you see it as a lesson. Reflect on the root causes and store these insights for future reference. By turning each bad result into a stepping stone, you avoid repeating the same mistakes.

19.12 Participating in Mentoring Circles or Peer Groups

Another option for continuous improvement is to join or form a group where negotiators share experiences. Such circles might meet monthly to discuss real negotiation stories—both wins and losses. This peer setting can:

- **Provide Diverse Perspectives**: Each member has unique backgrounds and can suggest solutions you never considered.
- **Offer Mutual Support**: When one member struggles with a stubborn client or a personal conflict, the group can brainstorm approaches.
- **Hold You Accountable**: Committing your improvement goals in front of peers can motivate you to follow through.

Look for local business clubs, online forums, or professional associations. If none exists, consider starting one with colleagues or friends who have an interest in building negotiation skills.

19.13 Tracking Trends and Reading Widely

Staying informed about broader trends can keep your negotiation style current. For example, if a new technology disrupts your industry's supply chain, you might need to renegotiate terms with partners. Regular reading of business magazines, market reports, or reputable blogs can alert you to changes before they catch you by surprise.

Additionally, reading biographies or case studies of great negotiators (in business, politics, or community work) can spark new ideas. Observing how they overcame deadlocks or navigated cultural barriers can inspire you to try new methods. Be curious: if something stands out, note it in your journal as a technique to test when the right moment comes.

19.14 Handling Different Personalities Better Over Time

Continuous improvement also means recognizing patterns in how you deal with various personality types. For instance:

1. **Aggressive Types**: Over time, you learn which calm responses or boundary-setting phrases consistently defuse tension.
2. **Overly Friendly Types**: You discover how to ensure that charm does not lead you to neglect your own needs.
3. **Vague Types**: Repeated encounters teach you how to ask probing questions that force clarity.

By noticing these personality-based patterns, you can build a toolkit of responses. This helps you handle new negotiators with similar traits more confidently.

19.15 Balancing Work and Personal Negotiations

Every negotiation, whether professional or personal, is a chance to refine your approach. If you only apply advanced tactics at work, you miss practice opportunities in daily life—like deciding vacation plans or sorting out expenses with friends. Conversely, your personal experiences can teach valuable lessons for work deals (like how to stay calm or find creative compromises).

That said, keep in mind the differences in stakes and relationships. A method that works with colleagues might need toning down at home to maintain harmony, and vice versa. But each sphere can still inform the other, building your adaptability.

19.16 The Role of Reflection After Each Talk

Reflection should be immediate enough that details are fresh in your mind but not so rushed that you fail to see the big picture. A simple approach after each negotiation:

1. **Take a Quiet Moment**: Even five minutes alone to jot down notes or mentally replay key points.
2. **Ask Yourself**: "What did I do well? What surprised me? What could I improve next time?"
3. **Store the Learning**: If you keep a digital or paper journal, record the insights.
4. **Look Ahead**: Is there a similar negotiation coming soon? How might you apply these lessons right away?

This process cements what you have learned and prevents you from forgetting important takeaways in the hustle of daily tasks.

19.17 Avoiding Overconfidence

As you gain skill, there is a risk of becoming complacent or arrogant. Overconfidence can lead to careless preparation or underestimating the other side. A few signs of overconfidence:

- **Skipping Basic Research**: Assuming you already know enough to wing it.
- **Ignoring Feedback**: Brushing off constructive criticism with "I know what I'm doing."
- **Treating Others Poorly**: Believing you are always the smartest in the room, so you can bully or dismiss them.

Continuous improvement requires humility. Remember that each negotiation is unique. A small shift in context—like a new competitor or a different personality—can challenge your usual methods. Staying humble keeps you open to learning something new every time.

19.18 Golden Gem: Turn Every Setback into a Future Advantage

A practical gem for continuous improvement is to view setbacks or losses as raw material for progress. For instance, if a negotiation fell apart because you struggled with a cultural misunderstanding, you can research that culture's norms so deeply that next time you excel at cross-cultural deals. If you parted ways with a potential client because you failed to articulate your value, sharpen your pitch and practice until it feels effortless. In this way, each hurdle becomes the spark that propels you to a stronger level.

19.19 Pulling It All Together

Continuous improvement is not a formal course you take once—it is an attitude. It means:

- **Noticing** what happens in each negotiation.
- **Analyzing** your behavior and outcome.

- **Seeking** external viewpoints or data.
- **Setting** tangible goals for your growth.
- **Taking** steady action to refine your strategy.

Over time, these small, repeated steps build massive progress. You will gain confidence, adaptability, and the skills to handle even the trickiest talks. When you compare your present abilities to what they were a year ago, the difference can be enormous.

19.20 Conclusion

Negotiation is a lifelong practice. By focusing on continuous improvement, you ensure that every conversation, every minor deal, and every major agreement becomes a lesson. This helps you remain relevant in changing markets, fosters deeper relationships, and provides a foundation for success in both business and personal spheres.

Golden gem: Never see a negotiation as a finished story. Each outcome—good or bad—is a stepping stone to a more refined, more capable version of yourself. Keep learning, keep applying, and keep evolving.

With that, we have explored how to keep your negotiation skills alive and growing. In our final chapter (Chapter 20), we will look at real-world examples and final words of wisdom to cement the lessons from this entire guide. You will see how negotiation strategies apply in day-to-day life and in high-stakes settings alike, giving you practical takeaways to hold onto.

Chapter 20: Real-World Examples and Final Words

Throughout this book, we have covered the essentials of negotiation: goal-setting, research, communication, handling emotions, creative thinking, bargaining approaches, ethical standards, and the importance of continuous growth. In this final chapter, we will explore real-world scenarios that illustrate these principles in action. We will see how people from different walks of life have used these skills to navigate business deals, personal relationships, and cultural barriers.

After reviewing these examples, we will wrap up with key takeaways to keep in mind as you apply everything you have learned. You will see that negotiation is not a mysterious art reserved for certain personalities—it is an accessible set of methods and attitudes that anyone can develop. Let these final words encourage you to keep growing, experimenting, and refining your style as a negotiator.

20.1 Case Study 1: A Salary Negotiation

Context: Lisa, a software developer, has worked at her company for two years. She feels her responsibilities have grown significantly, yet her pay has not kept pace. She decides to negotiate a raise.

1. **Preparation**: Lisa gathers market data on typical developer salaries in her region and for her skill level. She also lists her contributions—like leading a small team on a recent project.
2. **Setting Objectives**: She sets a target salary range (with a minimum she will accept) and also notes alternative perks, like extra vacation, if the pay number is not possible.
3. **Communication**: Lisa approaches her manager politely, scheduling a dedicated meeting rather than bringing it up casually. She outlines her accomplishments and the industry benchmarks.
4. **Listening**: Her manager explains the company's budget constraints but acknowledges Lisa's value.

5. **Outcome**: After some discussion, the manager offers a raise slightly below her top figure but includes a one-time bonus and a plan to revisit her pay in six months.
6. **Reflection**: Lisa accepts, feeling the deal is reasonably fair, though not perfect. She notes that her clear research and respectful tone helped her manager see she was serious.

Lesson: This example shows how having facts at hand, plus setting realistic goals, can lead to a constructive conversation. Lisa's readiness to consider non-monetary perks also gave her manager room to compromise.

20.2 Case Study 2: A Small Business Partnership

Context: Daniel runs a local bakery that specializes in custom desserts. He wants to expand his reach by partnering with a popular coffee shop, owned by Maria, who also wants to offer unique baked items to customers.

1. **Research and Approach**: Daniel looks at the coffee shop's style and typical clientele. He prepares samples that match their brand image—like pastries with coffee-flavored frosting. Maria tries them and sees a potential boost to her morning sales.
2. **Negotiation Goals**: Daniel wants shelf space and brand visibility, with a fair profit share. Maria wants reliable deliveries, freshness, and consistent quality.
3. **Bargaining**: They talk about logistics (Daniel's daily delivery times, how many pastries to stock). Maria insists on a trial period before committing long-term.
4. **Creative Problem-Solving**: Daniel suggests Maria promote the new pastries on a special board for a month, then track sales. If they hit a certain target, they sign a six-month contract.
5. **Outcome**: After the trial, sales are good. They formalize a deal with a sliding scale: as pastry orders grow, Daniel's cut increases. Both sides are happy—Maria's coffee shop stands out, Daniel gets a stable distribution channel.
6. **Reflection**: They realize how a test phase can reduce risk and show real demand. By focusing on mutual benefit—coffee and pastries—they find a win-win structure.

Lesson: This scenario highlights the benefits of a pilot approach, aligning both parties' interests and removing fear of commitment. Clear aims, data tracking, and fair terms created a robust business relationship.

20.3 Case Study 3: A Family Dispute Over Chores

Context: In a household of four (two parents, two teenagers), chores have caused ongoing tension. Everyone feels the tasks are unfairly distributed. The parents want the teens to take more responsibility, while the teens argue they have heavy schoolwork.

1. **Preparation**: The parents list all weekly chores—laundry, grocery shopping, cooking, cleaning, etc. They note how much time each typically takes.
2. **Setting a Family Meeting**: They pick a calm weekend afternoon to talk. They highlight the need for a balanced approach to avoid resentment.
3. **Communication and Listening**: Each teenager shares their schedule, pointing out tough homework days. Parents explain the stress of handling too many chores alongside work.
4. **Brainstorming**: They make a chore chart, letting each teen pick tasks they find less burdensome. One teen prefers cooking over cleaning, the other is okay with vacuuming but hates washing dishes.
5. **Concessions and Agreement**: The parents agree to help sometimes with the bigger tasks if the teens maintain the smaller daily ones. Everyone decides to rotate certain chores monthly so no one gets stuck doing the same disliked task forever.
6. **Outcome**: The new plan is posted on the fridge. Each family member can see what they are responsible for. They set a mid-month check-in to review if it is working.
7. **Reflection**: Less conflict arises because tasks are clearly assigned and revolve. The teens feel more respected, and the parents feel some relief.

Lesson: This example underlines how open dialogue, shared input, and compromise can resolve everyday friction. By treating it like a real negotiation—listing tasks, hearing concerns, and agreeing on a schedule—families can keep the peace.

20.4 Case Study 4: A Cross-Cultural Business Deal

Context: A tech company based in the United States wants to license its software to a partner in Japan. Both sides value the deal, but they differ in how they communicate. The American side is used to direct talk and quick decisions, while the Japanese side prefers a more formal pace and group consensus.

1. **Preparation and Awareness**: The American negotiators read about Japanese business etiquette, learning that building rapport and respecting hierarchy matters. They approach the talks with politeness, exchanging small gifts.
2. **Early Discussions**: The Japanese team asks many clarifying questions and takes careful notes, but rarely says "No" outright. They use phrases like "We will consider this." The Americans realize this might mean partial disagreement.
3. **Adaptation**: Instead of pushing for immediate final decisions, the Americans break the negotiation into smaller steps, allowing the Japanese side to consult internally. This shows respect for their group approval process.
4. **Face-to-Face Meetings**: They hold a video conference where each side's senior representatives greet each other, signaling mutual respect. The Americans gently confirm key points: "Are you comfortable with a three-year license at this rate?"
5. **Outcome**: After multiple sessions, they finalize a contract that includes a rollout schedule and quality assurances. The Japanese side appreciates the Americans' patience and clarity, while the Americans are glad they took the time to adapt.
6. **Reflection**: Both teams note that bridging cultural gaps took extra effort. However, it built trust that might lead to further expansions or joint ventures later.

Lesson: Cross-cultural talks often require patience, respect for hierarchy, and careful reading of indirect signals. Adapting to the other side's style can unlock deals that might fail under more aggressive, rushed methods.

20.5 Reviewing the Book's Core Lessons

Over the chapters, we have covered:

1. **Basics of Negotiation** (Chapter 1): Understanding what negotiation is and how it appears in daily life.
2. **Setting Clear Objectives** (Chapter 2): Deciding your goals, fallback plans, and priorities.
3. **Research and Information Gathering** (Chapter 3): Preparing factual data and understanding the other side's background.
4. **Preparation Tools and Techniques** (Chapter 4): Checklists, role-playing, and planning strategies.
5. **Communication Fundamentals** (Chapter 5): Clarity, tone, and how to deliver your message effectively.
6. **Listening Skills** (Chapter 6): Active listening to spot hidden needs and signals.
7. **Body Language in Negotiations** (Chapter 7): Reading and controlling nonverbal cues.
8. **Building Trust and Credibility** (Chapter 8): Honesty, consistency, and respect that form a strong base.
9. **Handling Emotions and Conflict** (Chapter 9): Staying calm, resolving disputes, and not letting anger derail talks.
10. **Creative Problem-Solving** (Chapter 10): Generating fresh ideas and flexible solutions.
11. **Approaches to Bargaining** (Chapter 11): Methods like anchoring, first offers, and concession tactics.
12. **Understanding Cultural Differences** (Chapter 12): Navigating norms across various regions and groups.
13. **Negotiations in Business** (Chapter 13): Applying these skills in contracts, salary talks, and company deals.
14. **Negotiations in Personal Life** (Chapter 14): Using respectful dialogue for chores, finances, or social matters.

15. **Handling Difficult Negotiators** (Chapter 15): Managing bullies, liars, and aggressive players with calm and boundaries.
16. **Tactics to Avoid** (Chapter 16): Steering clear of unethical tricks that harm trust.
17. **Ethical Standards in Negotiation** (Chapter 17): Building a lasting reputation through honesty and fairness.
18. **Technology and Digital Negotiation** (Chapter 18): Embracing new tools while keeping personal warmth.
19. **Continuous Improvement** (Chapter 19): Reflecting, learning, and evolving your style.

These chapters form a comprehensive guide, each piece supporting the others. Negotiation is a broad topic, but if you apply these core ideas step by step, you can become a more confident and effective negotiator.

20.6 Frequently Asked Questions (FAQ)

Q1: What if the other side refuses to negotiate and insists on their terms?

- You can calmly explain why their terms might not be acceptable. Ask open questions to see if there is any flexibility. If they remain unmoving, consider your backup plan. Sometimes walking away is the wise choice.

Q2: Can I negotiate if I am shy or introverted?

- Absolutely. Introverts can be excellent at researching, listening carefully, and thinking before speaking. You do not need to be loud to be successful; you just need clarity, preparation, and respectful communication.

Q3: How do I deal with regret if I think I agreed too quickly?

- Take it as a lesson. Next time, set a personal rule to ask for a brief pause or to confirm details before finalizing. If the deal is not yet signed, you can politely request a reconsideration, though that might harm trust if you do it repeatedly.

Q4: Are there times when negotiation is inappropriate?

- In emergencies (like life-or-death scenarios), immediate action might matter more than bargaining. Also, some regulated areas (public fees, standard tariffs) might have less room for haggling. Know the context before pushing to negotiate.

Q5: Can negotiation improve my relationships outside of business?

- Yes. Good negotiation skills—listening, empathy, fairness—strengthen all kinds of relationships, from marriage to friendships to community work. It is about reaching agreements that work for everyone.

20.7 Final Words of Encouragement

Negotiation is not a distant skill that only lawyers or executives use. Every day, you face situations where you and others want different things. By learning to talk about these differences calmly, gather relevant facts, and explore possible solutions, you create outcomes that feel balanced and fair. Even small steps, like asking clarifying questions or recognizing emotional triggers, can make a huge difference.

Remember that no one is perfect at negotiation from the start. It is normal to make mistakes, to occasionally accept less than you deserve, or to let frustration slip out. Treat these moments as part of your learning path. Each talk is a chance to refine your approach and become more comfortable speaking up for yourself and understanding the needs of others.

20.8 A Glance at Future Possibilities

As the world keeps changing, negotiation skills will remain valuable. You might face new challenges like remote work, digital transactions, or emerging market shifts. Staying flexible and open-minded lets you handle these developments smoothly. Whether you negotiate pay in a new job, sign a contract with an international partner, or discuss responsibilities in a shared household, the same basic principles apply:

- **Clarity** about what you want.
- **Honesty** and respect for the other side's viewpoint.
- **Preparedness** to explain why your offer is reasonable.
- **Willingness** to explore creative middle ground.
- **Calm** under pressure.

With these foundations, you can feel at ease even when big or unexpected questions arise.

20.9 Your Personal Call to Action

Now that you have read this entire guide, how can you put it to work?

1. **Pick One Upcoming Negotiation**: Maybe you have a small conversation or a bigger deal on the horizon. Decide to apply at least two concepts from the book—such as better research, an opening offer strategy, or improved listening.
2. **Review**: After it is over, spend a few minutes writing down what went well and what could be improved.
3. **Rinse and Repeat**: Keep doing this with each new situation. Over time, you will see a clear upward path in your competence.

If you stay active and mindful, these techniques will not remain theory. They will blend into your daily habits, giving you a lasting advantage in all sorts of interactions.

20.10 Golden Gem and Conclusion

Negotiation is a skill you can keep refining for a lifetime. Whether dealing with a complex business merger or figuring out the weekend plans with friends, the same underlying logic—communicate clearly, listen actively, solve problems respectfully—leads to better results. You do not need to be confrontational or manipulative to do well. You just need to approach each dialogue as a constructive exchange, where both sides can find ways to satisfy their key interests.

Golden gem: Always leave the door open for future talks. Even if you cannot reach an agreement today, a respectful approach ensures you can talk again tomorrow. Burning bridges by being rude or dishonest can cut off possibilities you might need later.

Thank you for going through this entire journey on "How to Negotiate: A Comprehensive Guide to Successful Negotiations." You now have a wide range of tools: from setting precise objectives and conducting thorough research, to handling emotions, building trust, and harnessing technology safely. Remember that negotiation is part art, part science, and part personal growth process. Keep learning, stay curious, and continue shaping your approach to fit each situation. In doing so, you will not only achieve better deals but also form stronger, more respectful relationships in all areas of life.

www.ingramcontent.com/pod-product-compliance
Lightning Source LLC
LaVergne TN
LVHW012043070526
838202LV00056B/5579